Immigrant on Earth

Immigrant on Earth

A Philosopher on the Road to Emmaus

OCTAVIAN GABOR

RESOURCE *Publications* · Eugene, Oregon

IMMIGRANT ON EARTH
A Philosopher on the Road to Emmaus

Copyright © 2025 Octavian Gabor. All rights reserved. Except for brief quotations in critical publications or reviews, no part of this book may be reproduced in any manner without prior written permission from the publisher. Write: Permissions, Wipf and Stock Publishers, 199 W. 8th Ave., Suite 3, Eugene, OR 97401.

Resource Publications
An Imprint of Wipf and Stock Publishers
199 W. 8th Ave., Suite 3
Eugene, OR 97401

www.wipfandstock.com

PAPERBACK ISBN: 979-8-3852-3525-4
HARDCOVER ISBN: 979-8-3852-3526-1
EBOOK ISBN: 979-8-3852-3527-8

VERSION NUMBER 032625

Contents

Prologue | ix

A Rabbit and My Involuntary Participation in Ugliness | 1
A Tree on a Country Road | 3
What Is Your Use for This World? | 5
Moments of Life with Neil Diamond | 8
Beauty in Anonymity | 10
Our Images in Other People's Worlds | 12
Sunday Walk to Golgotha | 15
Places of Regeneration | 17
Oases of Freedom | 18
Departures | 20
An Aching Love | 21
Forgiveness Sunday | 22
Immigrant Story | 24
The Icons Formed by Others in My Soul | 26
Coming Together as a Nation in a Narcissistic World | 28
Thoughts in the Air | 32
Two Kinds of Expectation | 35
Angels and Birth-givers | 37
Stories from Communism | 38
What Would I Have Done | 40
Afraid to Be in Heaven | 42

Identity Stories | 44
Praise and the Evil Eye | 46
The Restoration of Memory as Public Sacrament | 48
Some Thoughts on Levinas and Orthodoxy | 50
The Church and the Problem of the Third | 54
Laughter, Levinas, and the Otherwise than Being | 56
Nothing to Be Done: Waiting for Godot | 61
We Are All to Blame | 63
I Am a Nobody for Whom Someone Is on a Cross | 66
The Pigs Who "Took" the Light | 68
Losing Yourself in the Depths of Your Being | 69
Pregnant with the Beautiful | 72
Radical Diversity and C. S. Lewis | 75
The Spring of Love | 78
The Temptation to Change the Suffering of the World | 80
Healing Responsibility | 82
Mercy and Pity | 84
The Two Old Men | 85
The Legend of Manole and Ana: Building a Church in One's Bones | 89
Giving Thanks for Shortcomings | 91
It Sounds Like Reason, except that It Was a Choice | 93
A Lonely Superhuman with Simple Arithmetic | 96
"There Was No Other Choice" | 98
"Christ Is Risen!" Now . . . What? | 102
Ode to My Wife | 104
The Canon of Joy | 106
Hoarders of Ideas | 109
Incomplete Morning Thought on Heaven | 113
Time and Eternity | 114
The Gift of Failure | 117

The Situation of the Earth | 126
Beyond Morality | 132
Daily Involuntary Participation in Ugliness | 134
Moments of Travel with Dostoevsky and Elder Cleopa | 137

Bibliography | 141

Prologue

THIS BOOK CAME TO be by itself, without any plans. It brings together writings over a span of eight years. It began without any end in sight. My writing went in various directions, witnessing various tribulations or thoughts that visited me during these travels that compose life. Life seems to be a journey toward a place fully known and unknown at the same time. There is one certitude about human beings: we all die, and our existence as we know it has an end. But there is also the unknowability of what takes place, if anything, after this end.

This completely known and unknown end governs our journeys here. It also makes us immigrants, in more than one way. In this book, a Romanian lives in the United States, a philosopher belongs to the body of the Church, an Orthodox Christian lives in a Christian world where Orthodoxy is in minority. But beyond these particularities, we all come to dwell in a place that precedes us and will survive us. We come as travelers into a place for which we had done nothing, and we leave behind us a place whose flavor is influenced by our bodies. We do not travel alone, but with others; at times, they are alive only on the pages of a book. Most of the time, they are our contemporaries, in flesh and blood. Our communications with these people can be described as attempts to apply for visas to be accepted into their souls.

This book is also such an application for visas into your souls. Each one of you, its readers, will decide whether to offer it or not.

Prologue

I want to thank everyone who has read the manuscript and offered me guidance. My wife, Elena Gabor, has provided feedback from the initial phases of writing. Stefan Cojocaru, Caryl Emerson, Adrian Nicolae Guiu, and Dana LaCourse Munteanu provided helpful suggestions and called me on lack of clarity. Beyond their help with the text, their friendships are some of the most precious gifts life has offered me.

In January 2025, I had a one-month fellowship at the Bogliasco Center, on the miraculous Ligurian coast of Italy. I am grateful to the center for giving me the chance of completing this book.

A Rabbit and My Involuntary Participation in Ugliness

I WAS WALKING IN the neighborhood. A rabbit got scared, ran into the street, and got hit by a car. It was part of my daily involuntary participation in ugliness.

I heard two things at the same time: the muffled sound ending the rabbit's life and the voice in my head justifying that I was not responsible. I had no intention of scaring the rabbit, and I rejoiced when I first saw him. By all accounts, I seemed morally and legally not guilty. I am not guilty.

But the voice soon got silenced. It was the echo of the muffled sound of the car that silenced it, although the car was already far away. In the silence I experienced, I remembered my non-moral responsibility. I do participate in this world, and by my participation I contribute to its ugliness. It is not about cause and effect; this is just how things are. In this world, fallen as it is, ugliness takes place everywhere, and my example with the rabbit is insignificant if we compare it with tragedies all over the place. However, the rabbit story is part of it. The rabbit and I are ingredients of the large soup that the world is (I heard this analogy between the world and the soup someplace, but I don't remember who said it). My belonging to it makes me part of its beauty and of its ugliness: I contribute to the taste of this soup. And since I participate in ugliness most of the time, regardless of whether I want it or not, I need forgiveness. It is not a moral or juridical forgiveness but rather a curative one. If the world suffers and I am part of it, then the world and I need to be cured. Ugliness as disease took place this morning, when the rabbit died. Ugliness as disease takes place when we harm others. Asking for forgiveness is asking to be with the world in its healing process.

When he saw me walking, the rabbit did not come to me but ran away: the symptom of brokenness, ugliness, and separation. Forgive me, little rabbit.

A Tree on a Country Road

A COUNTRY ROAD. A tree.

The setting of Beckett's *Waiting for Godot*[1] matches the condition of travelers we have on this earth. We are on a road. We don't remember where it began, and we are not responsible for starting it. The only thing we can do as long as we are alive is to continue traveling on this road. We don't know what will take place while walking, but we are given the certainty of a tree. Just like the travelers from Aesop's fable:

> *Around noon on a summer's day, some travellers who were exhausted by the heat caught sight of a plane tree. They went and lay down in the shade of the tree in order to rest. Looking up at the tree, they remarked to one another that the plane tree produced no fruit and was therefore useless to mankind. The plane tree interrupted them and said, "What ungrateful people you are! You denounce my uselessness and lack of fruit at the very moment in which you are enjoying my kindness!"*[2]

Is Aesop's fable a key to Beckett's play? We are on a road, traveling toward Godot, waiting for Godot to make his apparition by giving us some fruit, while a tree is next to us, and we don't even pay attention to it.

Beckett's country road is the road to Emmaus. The tree is the presence that we take for granted. We walk on the road to Emmaus

---

1. Beckett, *Waiting for Godot*, 1.
2. *Aesop's Fables*, 43.

next to the Plane Tree and explain to Him everything that has happened in our terms. We explain to Him *our* story about *His* life, and we are amazed that He, the Plane Tree, is the only one who doesn't know the story, who doesn't know that it's not sufficient to stand and litter the ground with leaves. It must bring forward fruit. And we tell Him, the Tree, what His fruit should be. All of this while walking toward the "end" of the path, an end that we "know." But there is no end of the path if we remain in the cooling shade of the Plane Tree being revealed in the breaking of the bread (Luke 24:30).

Verweile doch, du bist so schön![3]

"'I've been here all this time, and I will not run away,'" the Plane Tree would say. For the tree is a beautiful idiot, just like Dostoevsky's Prince Myshkin. An "idiot" who makes no sense, who cannot justify his existence. And we want to feast on his body, just as we want to feast on the fruit of the plane tree. Still, an "idiot" does not run away but offers himself to others despite the evidence that this offering brings about no positive result, despite the fact that our eyes are still not open. And we feast on his body. Some do it in thanksgiving. Others, like the travelers from Aesop's fable and even Estragon and Vladimir from Beckett's play, do it without even acknowledging it.

Can we become plain trees that offer shade on the road to Emmaus? Can we become trees which, instead of offering fruit to others, offer themselves? There's such a long way from an ungrateful traveler under a plane tree to a plane tree. It is the way from obliviousness to thankfulness.

---

3. "Stay, you are so beautiful!" In German, from Goethe's *Faust*.

What Is Your Use for This World?

AT THE BEGINNING OF his *The Karamazov Brothers*, Dostoevsky asks a question that may come naturally in a utilitarian world: "Why would I, the reader, spend my time studying the history of his life?" The "hero" Dostoevsky writes about is Alyosha. The Russian writer knows that there is nothing remarkable about his hero. Alyosha is "of indeterminate character, whose mission is undefined."[1] The question comes naturally: what is your use for this world, Alyosha Karamazov?

In our contemporary world, governed by usefulness, this is a question we all face. And the answer has to be given here and now. It must follow a rubric. And it must be assessable. The world asks you constantly to justify your existence. The world asks you to be of a determinate character. To take upon yourself a feature, any feature, so it can judge you and pin you on a map of meaning. Who are you, Alyosha Karamazov? In the absence of a definition that makes sense to the world, your indetermination becomes itself a determination from the perspective of the world. The odd, the indeterminate, those who do not fall into our normal categories, those who are neither "friends" nor "enemies," trouble us. They challenge our sentiment of justice, because we lack the categories according to which we can "reward" them. The easiest way to deal with them is to give them a determination: we make them "the exiled."

---

1. Dostoevsky, *Karamazov Brothers*, 5.

This often happens to philosophy on today's campuses. Philosophy is the hunchback of medieval times: send it to the outskirts of the city, for we can find no use of it in a world in which the heroes are masters of dealing with black and white. It is the revenge of the sophists and bad poets who, after Plato told them they have no place in his republic, have come with definitions and reorganized it. In this place, we need answers now. Alyosha gives no immediate answers. Philosophy gives no immediate answers. So we plunge ourselves into the cold world of monetary value that gives an answer in the now. Philosophy departments? Too expensive for today's academic world, and their outcomes are not immediately measurable. What is your use for this world, Alyosha Karamazov?

Of course, the world "values" individuals. But what the world means by individuals are clearly defined beings who belong to a category: the world values the individuals' determinations. If they do not belong to categories, we rush to find one for them, to place them on our maps, our worlds. But you, Alyosha Karamazov? You, the man of indeterminate character, what is your use for this world? You, Socrates, what is your use for this world? You, philosophy department, what is your use for this world?

After he points out that Alyosha Karamazov is a non-hero, Dostoevsky immediately brings about a new topic, the real book about Alyosha. *The Karamazov Brothers*, even if it is about an indeterminate hero (or perhaps precisely because it is about an indeterminate hero), is merely the first volume of a larger project, he says. "I have one life story and two novels. The second novel is the main one; this concerns my hero's actions right up to the present time."[2]

Dostoevsky did not write a second volume. Even if he may have planned to do so, Dostoevsky could not have written a book in which Alyosha is a determinate hero because it would have

---

2. Dostoevsky, *Karamazov Brothers*, 6.

transformed Alyosha into a type. Instead, Alyosha haunts his readers, just as Dostoevsky's book does. The second book, while it is Dostoevsky's, is not only his: it is the volume that comes to be in his readers' hearts, which takes place every moment, "right up to the present time." It so happens when someone dwells in your heart: the relationship you have with him is renewed at every instance.

I remember Aesop's fable, the one with two travelers walking in the noonday sun, seeking the shade of a tree to rest. They saw a plane tree and rested in its shadow. "How useless is the plane tree," they said. It bears no fruit and only serves to litter the ground with leaves. All of this while resting in its cooling shade

What is your use, Alyosha Karamazov?

What is your use, Socrates?

What is your use, philosophy departments across the world?

We will discover it when they stop giving birth to beauty in our hearts.

Moments of Life with Neil Diamond

I HAVE THE FEELING I forgot something in the hotel room. And I am bothered by the fact that I couldn't check in for my flight. "We could not reserve seats for all passengers. You need to check in at the airport." Bummer! I need to get to the airport fast, to solve the problem, so a little bit of stress takes a hold of me.

"Good morning!" The driver of the shuttle is in his seventies, the age of my dad. I'm not good enough with accents to realize which part of the US he is from, but there's something warm in the song of his voice. "Sunday morning!" he says. "Easy drive today, we'll be there in twenty minutes."

"Did I really forget something in the hotel room?"

There are no other passengers in the shuttle. We make a U-turn, and the driver starts a CD. And my life changes: it's Neil Diamond's "Sweet Caroline." The driver sings along. His voice is really warm. There's a force pulling me, too, and I can no longer hold it. Two strangers singing together in an airport shuttle, touching each other's souls through the melody and verses of the song.

I forget that I forgot something in the hotel room: *Sweet Caroline!*

"Do you like singing?" I ask him. "Oh, yeah! I used to run corporate parties. I did the forty-five minutes Elvis routine. I had a ball doing that." He had some problems a few years ago with his vocal cords, and he had to stop.

I don't know his name. He probably knows mine from the ticket. Still, it's brother love.

We arrived at the airport, and I haven't checked the time once. "A good day sir!" he says. "It's Sunday."

I forgot my phone charger in the hotel room.

Let's fly! It's a good day to die.

Beauty in Anonymity

I WAKE UP EARLY, and I witness moments of remarkable beauty. A dawn that still allows the moon to be seen above a cloud, sun rays breaking through the branches of a tree . . . moments that I would have missed if I had not woken up. Moments that so many other people miss, and not only because they are not awake at this hour but because they work, they live in other parts of the world, or simply because they see other moments of beauty which I cannot see.

There is so much beauty in the world that happens in a second, regardless of whether we see it or not. Beauty in anonymity. Of course, there are those private moments we occasion for one another, in the anonymity of our lives: the caress of a grandmother for a child, the smile of a parent when a daughter takes her first steps, or the serene forehead of your wife while sleeping next to you in the early hours of the day. Moments of which nobody else is aware, perhaps not even those who allow you to have them.

We create all these moments for one another, and we are aware of their uniqueness: we even desire them to be unique. The caress is for me and no one else. But what about a sunset or a dawn? For "my" dawn this morning would not have happened if I chose to sleep in. The sun would have still risen, of course, and the moon could still be seen, people may have rejoiced in it, but that particular moment in which the beauty of the dawn took life in my soul would have missed its conception.

The world is indeed beautiful. And it is beautiful in anonymity, just as forgiveness is always there, always with its arms stretched on a cross, waiting for me to come for an embrace.

Beauty does save the world. And it does so anonymously.

Our Images in Other People's Worlds

THERE IS SOMETHING TROUBLING in the idea that people live in their own world, in which I belong as a constituent, a world different than mine (I am not a character in my own world, but I am a character in their worlds): it raises the problem of my responsibility for all because I belong to their worlds. I don't have to listen to me, to wait behind me in line at a supermarket, or to deal with me as my spouse or as a driver on the highway. All other people with whom I interact somehow need to "deal" with me, depending on the relations established between us. Thus, I am responsible for their worlds. At the same time, it is not really "me" who belongs to their world, and this is due to the way in which people see their own lives, the kind of orientation they have.

There is one more level, though: how responsible am I for the image that is created in the discourses other people have about me or about what I say? Consider it this way: Mary and Johnny have a discussion, and Johnny describes something I said, but this description is filtered by Johnny's own emotions and interests. Mary is thus hurt by "my" comments as they were described by Johnny. Am I responsible for Mary's feelings?

The first response—and this is the response most people would give—is that Johnny has responsibility for what he says. I have done nothing. First, the description of my words is out of context. Second, I have not intended to say something that could have harmed Mary. Thus, Johnny is exclusively responsible for any harm Mary may have suffered.

However, the event involves me, regardless of whether I contribute to it voluntarily or not. My problem is not whether Johnny is responsible for what Johnny does: this is Johnny's problem; my problem is how I contribute to his life and, by consequence, to Mary's life. The paradox is that I am responsible even if I have no control over his decision to talk to Mary. Johnny belongs to a world in which I am a component.

The prayer before communion: I believe, O Lord, and I confess that You are truly the Christ, the Son of the Living God, Who came into the world to save sinners, of whom I am the first.

People hear "responsibility" and believe this is a "moralist" approach. It is not, however, a moral responsibility, but the expression of the acknowledgement that I leave a trace in this world, for the good and for the bad. Regardless of my intentions, what I say or do can be interpreted, used, or truncated. I am an ingredient in this wonderful soup that life is. And I cannot complain about its taste. Belonging to it makes me part of its beauty and of its ugliness; it makes me part of its taste. Since I participate in ugliness most of the time, regardless of whether I want it or not, I need cleansing, which is forgiveness. It is not the moral or juridical forgiveness but rather the curative one. If the world suffers and I am part of it, then the world and I need to be cured.

Perhaps everything that happens to us is, if we read it well, another call to humility. I cannot say it better than Anthony Bloom:

> To me, humility is not what we often make of it: the sheepish way of trying to imagine that we are the worst of all and trying to convince others that our artificial

ways of behaving show that we are aware of that. Humility is the situation of the earth. The earth is always there, always taken for granted, never remembered, always trodden on by everyone, somewhere we cast and pour out all the refuse, all we don't need. It's there, silent and accepting everything and in a miraculous way making out of all the refuse new richness in spite of corruption, transforming corruption itself into a power of life and a new possibility of creativeness, open to the sunshine, open to the rain, ready to receive any seed we sow and capable of bringing thirtyfold, sixtyfold, a hundredfold out of every seed.[1]

And Mitya Karamazov comes to mind: "Gentlemen, we are all cruel, we are all monsters, we all cause suffering to people—to mothers and their infants—but, have it your way, I'm worse than anyone."[2]

Another paradox: this is an occasion for joy!

---

1. Bloom, *Beginning to Pray*, 35.
2. Dostoevsky, *Karamazov Brothers*, 641.

Sunday Walk to Golgotha

IN HIS *THE SACRED AND THE Profane*, Mircea Eliade speaks of the break in space brought about by what connects individuals with the divine. For the majority of peoples, the place of worship provides this separation. It is the Center of the World, from which humans take their own being. And so, Eliade says, "the religious man sought to live as near as possible to the center of the world."[1] The Center of the World, the place of worship, "is precisely the place where a break in plane occurs, where space becomes sacred, hence pre-eminently *real*."[2] Thus, in traditional villages, the church is placed in the middle, and all the other houses are built around it. The reality of each one of the villagers, their being, but also the being of their own dwellings depend on communication (perhaps communion) with the divine. The fortified churches of Transylvania provide plenty of examples for this.

"The centrality of the church does not appear everywhere," a friend of mine recently told me. "In my region, in Moldova, churches are built on a hill. When you go to church on Sunday morning, you go up the hill, just as you walk to Golgotha. You don't just go to church, but you are ascending there, you make an effort to be there. Those walks with my grandma when I was a child are more memorable to me than what happened during the service."

---

1. Eliade, *Sacred*, 43.
2. Eliade, *Sacred*, 45.

It is a different manifestation of the same attitude toward the sacred. We still have the break in space, but this time with a new aspect. The sacred is not only separated; now it also requires a journey. The same road was taken for burials, since cemeteries were also placed on the hill. It may be a suggestion that our lives are such journeys to Golgotha, the final destination. But it may also be a delicate understanding of Christianity that gives us a Kingdom which is already present but still not fully here, and thus we take a walk to Golgotha, to death, on every Sunday of the resurrection.

Places of Regeneration

THERE ARE CERTAIN PLACES in this world which have healing power. Some of them are spatial; others are temporal. Alyosha Karamazov was remembering his mother's face while praying: this is also a place of healing, even if it is the memory of a face in a relationship. Remembering it, being in its presence, does not allow you to think of bad things. The embrace of my grandma. I cannot judge people while I remember her embrace. A monastery: peace penetrating your bones.

In my experience, all these places have one feature in common: you are loved.

Preserve the places of regeneration of this world. Which may also mean, "become a place of regeneration for others." And this may mean: "embrace whoever is in your presence."

Oases of Freedom

THERE ARE TWO CONDITIONS for constituting an oasis of freedom for others. First, you have to stand for something, so others know where you are. Second, you have to embrace others as persons, regardless of where they are in life, and so accept them fully without any rest. The second condition is usually championed by all. The first condition, though, is often perceived in contradiction with the idea of not accepting others' freedom to act or be as they please. How can you say that you accept all, some may say, if you also claim that you have certain values? Don't these values encourage you to reject those who do not live by them?

If you have the first condition without the second, then you may likely reject others. My question, though, is whether the second has any meaning in the absence of the first. What kind of embrace is the one who comes from absence of values? What worth does it have? If you do not stand for anything, your embrace seems to be a meaningless act: it takes place in the absence of being. But there is so much meaning in the embrace of those who take you in their arms despite of all the reasons they have to reject you.

There is one character in Dostoevsky's works who lives his life as an oasis of freedom for others: Alyosha Karamazov, in whose presence all have "moments of goodness," as his father remarks, because all feel free to be who they are, regardless of their wickedness. They find rest in him, because there's no judgment in him. This doesn't mean that Alyosha has no values. In fact, it is precisely because he has values, because he has standards, that people find rest in him. If he did not, he would be a non-place, a desert in which you cannot quench your thirst, a meaningless desert without an oasis (a difference in a desert) in which you can find being.

Alyosha's values do not fix him; they give him an orientation. This is because he knows that he's never alone. "No individual can be existentially alone," Caryl Emerson writes about Bakhtin. "Values are already there and my task—or the task of my soul-to-be—is to attach to them. Thus an emerging self is not repressed by socialization (as in a Lacanian or Freudian model) but made whole through it."[1] Alyosha is always alive, authentic, not fixed into an ideology, but oriented toward values.

Perhaps this is another reason why the dialogue between Ivan and Alyosha is so rich. Ivan is the brother who has judgment. The way in which he understands freedom: if there is no God, everything is permitted. But such freedom is meaningless: the notion of "permitted" disappears. If there is no God, it is not as if everything is permitted or not; being allowed is no longer comprehensible. "Being embraced regardless of who you are" is meaningless. If there are no values beyond this horizontal existence, you cannot say that everything is permitted, because the notion of being permitted is no longer comprehensible.

Alyosha's notion of freedom: if there is God, everything is allowed. The notion of "everything" is not the same as it is in Ivan's statement. In God's presence, all things are different than they would be in his absence, because they already belong to God. If I begin with God, everything is permitted because I act within an embrace, and the embrace gives meaning beyond the phenomena. In Ivan, if there is no God, then everything is outside of God and outside of meaning: it no longer matters whether my actions cause harm.

Ivan allows all things, but he has no values. He wants to start with freedom outside of meaning. But in the absence of meaning, freedom and embrace are just as meaningless as anything else.

---

1. Emerson, "Mikhail Bakhtin," 616–17.

Departures

SOME OF MY FRIENDS are moving away these days. There's sadness around us but also moments of powerful feelings. The last liturgy in which we participate together; the last meal we share together; the last time when we say "see you tomorrow." All these moments of life take on new meaning, and, even if these separations are not happy events, they still give life some genuine force.

With time, like all of us, I have gotten used to my own departures—moments in which I die a little. This proximity of death, though, makes everything around me live. The leaf falling next to me vibrates its energy into my body; the driver showing signs of impatience is, nevertheless, participating in the final day I have in this space, and so his memory will come with me forever, tainted with this feeling of longing that dresses everything I experience into a warm light of eternity.

Can you imagine if we lived every moment of life as if it were our last one? If I looked into my wife's eyes as if it were the last time? If I sat around the table with my family as if it were our last dinner? If I opened the door for the cat to go out as if it were the last time I did so?

And I remember Fr. Cleopa who, when asked what the greatest wisdom in life was, answered, "Death! Death! Death!" Or live life as if it were your last moment.

An Aching Love

BEFORE I LEFT ROMANIA, I considered myself a citizen of the world. Once I left, I became the guy from Făgăraș, my hometown. I'm not talking about how other people saw me but rather about how I saw myself.

I live in the world and rejoice in its beauties, but I still bear the scars of my people. I bear their joys and sorrows. And I bear their history. My blood still boils when I remember Nușfalău, Treznea, or Fântâna Albă.[1] It's just a fact. It is as if I am these pains, even prior to being the current traveler. I'm not saying that my people are greater than others, but there is no place in the whole world where my heart aches more, where my heart lives more.

At times, people tell me I have no contact with reality. They say Romania has become for me some sort of icon, and so I don't perceive the real Romania, the one in which persons are treated by their governments as numbers (and, unfortunately, we got used to treating one another as numbers as well). And I think they are right: Romania has become an icon for me, but in a different sense: just like an icon makes the Kingdom somehow present, this icon makes me present. It connects me with myself.

I am in an airport, getting ready to leave again. In some sense, to live my earthly life. And still, why does it feel that I'm dying? Every time.

---

1. Places where Romanians were massacred by neighboring armies.

Forgiveness Sunday

I WENT TO CHURCH this morning, and I had to leave before Matins ended. I started to throw up. It smelt like cheese. Today is the last day of cheese, and I overindulged with it yesterday.

I came home and I crashed. I was a bit disappointed, since I really wanted to go to all Liturgies of the Triodion. But I guess learning how to fail is part of it.

When I woke up, I remembered it was the last day of cheese. So, regardless of how I felt in the morning, I ate a final piece of cheese. Then it dawned on me that I had to ask forgiveness from a friend of mine. I had not seen her in twenty years, but we had a discussion on Facebook, and I felt I harmed her. It was the occasion for a being-together with a friend.

Forgiveness vespers. Peace settles in.

> O Lord and Master of my life, take from me the spirit of sloth, despair, lust of power, and idle talk.
> But give rather the spirit of chastity, humility, patience, and love to Thy servant.
> Yea, O Lord and King, grant me to see my own transgressions, and not to judge my brother, for blessed art Thou, unto ages of ages. Amen. (The Lenten prayer of St. Ephraim).

"When we sin, we sin against God and the entire creation," the priest says at the end of the Vespers. People line up and ask forgiveness from one another. Young, old, men, women, priest, laity. And you see a child, a few years old, and ask forgiveness from him. Mitya's bairn . . .

> No, no, [. . .] tell me, why are those homeless mothers just standing there, why are the people so poor, why is the bairn so distressed, why are the steppes so bare, why don't they hug one another, why don't they kiss one another, why don't they sing joyful songs, why are they so ashen-faced and laden with so much despair and grief, why don't they feed the bairn?[1]

"Forgive me, a sinner!" the child tells me.
"God forgives and I forgive."
And so it begins.

---

1. Dostoevsky, *Karamazov Brothers*, 639.

Immigrant Story

THERE IS A MEDITERRANEAN grocery store in the town I live in. It is owned by a Syrian man. I do not know his story, but I think his family came to the US before the conflict started in Syria. Whenever I go to his store, I seem to have a back-in-the-past experience. Regardless of what he does at that moment, the owner, who is at the same time helping other people or doing what needs to be done, turns his head and greets me intently. I never have the impression that he is just doing his job. He takes me in, together with all the others, regardless of how busy he is. It feels as an acknowledgement that we are all together in the store and that the experience of each one of us is touched by the presence of each and all the others.

I have met various people in Saad's store. Many of them are immigrants. Many come from the Middle East—some of them are Muslims, others are Orthodox Christians, others are Catholics. People are not silent about what they believe in. They do not hide their identity and celebrate others. There is always joy in his store. I may feel this way because I find Romanian food. But I sometimes think it is because of Saad and his friendly countenance. He has an ability to take his customers into his care, making them feel no longer customer, but friends.

From time to time there is one more person in the store: Saad's father. He speaks no English, but he comes to you, shakes your hand with both of his hands, while looking straight into your eyes, saying, "good! good!" You have no idea what is good. But it is good. And he brings you something; first time we met, he made me a coffee. Today, he gave me an orange, an orange so fresh that it seemed he just got it from a tree. Then he comes back and shakes your hands again, still looking intently into your eyes. "Romania good, America good." Everything is good, and in Saad's store it truly seems like there is no evil in the world. When I left the store, he hugged me.

"I think he has seen things that are not so beautiful," my son said today, after we left the store. It may have been my impression, but I thought my son's eyes were wet. Same wetness that I see in the hard, resolved, but also warm and melancholic eyes of Saad's father.

The Icons Formed by Others in My Soul

A FRIEND OF MINE asked me once whether I would join a prayer group: we would each read a kathisma of the psalter per day during the Lenten periods.

I have no discipline in prayer, so I thought this would be a good occasion to build some. And I kept the rule well: I have not missed one day. But I often caught myself wandering in thought, losing focus, and uttering the psalms with my mouth but not with my soul.

From time to time, however, the words of prayer took life within me. It was not due to an increased level of concentration on my part. On the contrary, there was no connection with my ability to focus. Instead, it was due to others—and I have often discovered that everything good is so because others have brought it to life.

Today, for example, I was reading my kathisma, often losing the train of thought, when I discovered that I started to sing. I did not really know what I was singing and why, so I focused on the text and realized that it was Psalm 102. It felt as if the psalm found something in me and, while I was wandering in thought about what I would need to do tomorrow, it started to sing by itself.

One should not imagine it was something like the prayer of the heart, about whom the Holy Fathers speak, when your heart prays unceasingly without you. Far from it. But it could be described in this way: I had experienced beauty when I heard these words chanted, and they have thus remained within my soul.

Their icon was in me through one chant, and, when I pronounced them mindlessly, they found the icon and began singing of God by themselves.

The same thing takes place when I get to Psalm 33, although I do not sing it. This memory is not connected with a song. I watched a documentary on Fr. Ilie Cleopa's life, and he shouts the beginning of Psalm 33: "*Bine voi cuvânta pe Domnul în toată vremea.*" I wrote it in Romanian because this is how I hear it. And my heart shouts it, really, whenever my kathisma includes this psalm, even though I read it in English. Still, it is improper to say that my heart shouts it; perhaps it is better like this: it is shouted within me.

Even if *I* promised a kathisma per day, and even if *I* utter the words of a kathisma every day, I am not the one praying but rather those people who have formed icons within my soul. They wake me up from my indifference and bring me back to the present, to the word I utter, bringing it to life. Terrible thing, really, to become indifferent to what you do at the present moment and live instead in the realm of the future and so of the imaginary.

It may be this connection with people who have come before me that brings me back to the present. And yet, I can't avoid thinking that this phenomenon takes place even when the icons are not beautiful memories, when they are not living words, but rather ugly ones, and this ugliness is resurrected in us whenever we encounter a similar script . . .

We write in the souls of others, for the good or for the bad. I have much to thank for and much to ask forgiveness for.

Coming Together as a Nation in a Narcissistic World[1]

I HAVE FRIENDS WHO voted for Trump. Some of them were deeply hurt economically; others thought they no longer had a voice. I do not discuss whether they were entitled to feel this way. I would rather say that they were experiencing pain, and their vote was an expression of this pain. Now, they are deeply hurt that others do not see their pain, considering them racists and sexists, although they often speak against racism and sexism themselves.

I also have friends who voted for Clinton. Some of them were deeply hurt by the comments of the Republican candidate concerning women, minorities, or disabled persons. They believe words matter (and I also do), and they cannot understand how a man with such discourse can be elected president. Their wounds were deep during the election season because every malicious word came straight to their core. Now, they are deeply hurt because others, those who voted for Trump, do not see their pain, and they are certain that their pain cannot be understood.

How can we possibly "come together as a nation" in such conditions? How can we come together when there is so much pain? Together as what? As a body? Against what? Forgetting all our differences? Coming together to support views so foreign to us that make us sick?

In 1990, immediately after communism fell in Romania, Ion Rațiu, one man who had lived in the West, in England, came back

---

1. Written after the USA elections of 2016.

home and became one of the candidates for the presidential elections. He was mocked by many because of his very elegant way of talking and behaving toward others. I do not remember him ever responding in the same manner. With his always present bow tie, he just smiled and continued his work of educating people on what "being free" means. During one of the debates, he said something that many of us did not understand back then; he defined democracy: "The essential element of democracy is not who has the largest number of votes. This is not democracy. Democracy means an understanding that man is at the center of society, and all institutions are for man's sake. Democracy means that you listen to the other and then you reject his point of view. The quintessence of democracy is expressed in one phrase: 'I will fight to my last drop of blood for your right to not agree with me.' If we are able to do this, then we begin understanding what democracy means. My role, if I am not elected, will be to bring democracy in this country to the best of my abilities."

Ion Rațiu received 4.29 percent of the votes, but he remained in the history of Romania as the one who had the courage to tell the truth even if people were not able to hear him.

If we consider the definition of democracy above, we may see something that we have forgotten. In order for democracy to be healthy, we need to remember that the other, as wrong as he or she may be, is more important than me. His or her pain is more important than my pain. The only way in which I can be cured is by attempting, to the best of my ability, to take care of his or her wounds.

You may say, but how can we respond to bigotry? Perhaps by remembering that a soul who thinks this way is already in much more torment than I am.

The world is not divided into righteous people and wicked people. We are just people in pain, more or less muddled, as Alyosha tells his father in *The Brothers Karamazov*, or maybe covered with more or less mud. Or consider Solzhenitsyn: "Gradually it was disclosed to me that the line separating good and evil passes not through states, nor between classes, nor between political parties either—but right through every human heart—and through all human hearts."[2]

I cannot tell you that we should pay attention to the pains of others. I profoundly dislike moralizing. I most often have no idea what the right thing to do for me is, and this disqualifies me from giving moral advice to others. Even more, these days, the only thing I see is pain, regardless of who people voted for—yes, pain, even in those who celebrate Trump's victory. But since the world is still wicked, perhaps we don't embrace others without paying attention to their worldviews, but we embrace them only if they share *our* pain. This narcissism produces the best field on which tyrants and self-proclaimed saviors appear. If people elect someone like this, I am responsible for it, even if I may not participate in voting. How am I responsible? Well, it is because there is too much pain in the world that I have forgotten. But perhaps my disease, my forgetfulness, my narcissism, so my inability to perceive my neighbors' suffering, is largely enough spread in the world that wickedness is all around us. Perhaps these surreal elections would not have been possible if we were not so narcissistic, so in love with *our* pain, that we have forgotten the pain of others, and we have forgotten that pain, justified or not, is experienced as real pain.

Coming together as a nation? We are already in this together, not only as a nation but as the entire world. A body filled with diseases. But we cannot feel together as long as we believe that the disease is manifested in those who disagree with us only. The only way in which coming together makes sense to me is by taking care of the wounds of this body. And this happens when we forget our wounds and we try to understand and heal the suffering of those around us, whoever they may be and regardless of whether their pain is justified.

---

2. Solzhenitsyn, *Gulag Archipelago*, 615.

Nicolae Istrate, who spent many years in the Gulag, was contemplating the possibility of being a communist who would persecute others:

> I do not regret that I went through this experience of the prison. If I did not go through it, I may have been a totally different man. I may have become a communist, or who knows what other things I may have done. How can I know what I could have done . . . Who knows what may have happened to me if I did not go to prison? If I think about my situation before the first prison, when I was a school principal, I may have gotten married, joined the party . . .
>
> When I came back, I found all my colleagues who were like me, teachers, professors, those of the same age with me who had not been to prison—they were all party chiefs. They were already heroes of the socialist work, had cars and all kinds of things. I may have been the same way if I did not go to prison.[3]

Nicolae Istrate does not say that people are not responsible for their beliefs. He rather says that I am responsible for understanding them.

---

3. Monk Moise, *Do Not Avenge Us*, 312.

Thoughts in the Air

I HAVE FLOWN MANY times. However, whenever I board a plane, I still have the thought that this flight may be the last. This happens today as well. As in all similar occasions, I am somehow fine with this idea, and this is because of the situation I am in. I am together with these different people, the gentleman who has already fallen asleep, even before the takeoff, the young lady who looks dreamingly out the window, perhaps thinking about a boyfriend who was left behind, or the lady in front of me, who holds a smartphone in her very manicured hands, texting furiously to one, two, or many people at the same time. And I am especially together with the old African lady who sits next to me—I find out she is from Ghana—who holds her hand in prayer, chanting something in her language. She is in a somewhat different reality. She has spoken loudly on the phone, and she now chants in a peaceful, calming tone, seeming to place her life in the hands of the Almighty. So many different people with so many different problems, but at this moment, all together in a box ready to fly. It feels as if we are all one.

I open my book and read the first line from Aristotle's *Physics* 1.3. "We shall see that it is impossible for 'all things to be one.'" Aristotle argues with Parmenides and Melissus, but in my context the sentence surprises me and sounds differently. For indeed it is impossible for all things to be one, regardless of how much I feel one with the old lady from Ghana who sits next to me, who calls the flight attendant out of nowhere, even if he is speaking at the same time with someone else, two rows in front of us. Or who moves her legs in "my space," and not because she does not have space but rather because there seems to be no personal space for her. There is a certain genuineness in all her gestures. The social requirements of the West have not yet taken hold of her, and her chant is really beautiful, tempting. But my world is not her world, and her world is not mine.

There are many worlds in this world, just as there are many families in one family. I remember how, when I was studying communication in Romania, a long time ago, our professor Mihai Dinu pointed to the fact that brothers and sisters do not grow up in the same family. Of course, parents change through time, and the second child does not get the same parenting experience as the first. But there is one more aspect to it. My brothers live in a family in which *I* am one of the children. I do not live in that family. I do not need to deal with me as a brother. I deal with them but not with me.

The world is similar: in my world, I do not need to deal with "Tavi." I do not perceive my movements, and I do not need to avoid me when "Tavi" is in my way. There is no moment in which I serve myself at a restaurant, no moment in which I am my own teacher in class, no moment in which I am my own husband or my own father. All the others, though, have worlds in which I am a component. I am responsible for their worlds—they live life dealing with the noise I have created in their worlds.

Still in flight, so back to my readings. *De Anima* now. I am going to a conference on Greek philosophy, and I am writing a paper on *psyche* in Aristotle. "Soul is the being-fully-itself of a natural body that has life potentially." The lady next to me, the African from Ghana, is being-fully-human. She lives her human life in her particular way. She chants, pushes me with her elbows, moves her legs under the seat in front of me, and I have difficulties writing. I have to move my body to avoid hitting her with my elbow when I write, but this brings me too close to my other neighbor, too westernized to suffer physical proximity. I am slightly bothered by the situation, and I almost desire to push her back with my elbow, to create some space for my writing. How terrible I must have become if I am bothered by the particular expression of being what I also am, a human! I, one manifestation in the world of being-fully-human, am bothered by another manifestation in the world of being fully human. I am bothered by me!

You may remember Raskolnikov from Dostoevsky's *Crime and Punishment*, the one who has "the old unpleasant feeling of exasperated dislike of any person who violated, or even seemed desirous of disturbing his privacy."[1] I am bothered by the old African lady's life. Am I not a potential Raskolnikov? Where are you, Sonya, to seize me by the shoulders, to yell at me, "Go at once, this instant, stand at the cross-roads, first bow down and kiss the earth you have desecrated, then bow to the whole world, to the four corners of the earth, and say aloud to all the world: 'I have done murder.'"[2]

I am coming back from the conference. Different plane, different people, different worlds. I have a whole row for myself! Two empty seats next to me! It really makes me happy. No other person: I can write, sleep, I can do whatever I want to do! But then I remember the old African lady, with her flowery dress, her chanting, and her old, wrinkled hands. They remind me of the hands of my *mama-mare* (grandmother). If she were next to me, I would kiss them, and I would thus kiss the earth that I have desecrated.

---

1. Dostoevsky, *Crime and Punishment*, 10.
2. Dostoevsky, *Crime and Punishment*, 403.

Two Kinds of Expectation

CHRISTOS YANNARAS FINDS IN the etymology of the word prosopon (person) a referential reality. "The preposition pros ('towards') together with the noun ôps (ôpos in the genitive), which means 'eye,' 'face,' 'countenance,' form the composite word prosopon: I have my face turned towards someone or something."[1] As humans, we live oriented toward something else. We often spend our moments by waiting for something to happen. When we are in school, we wish to be done and go home, or we wish to graduate and truly "start life." If we "start life," we want to finally have money and so the freedom to do what we like. If it's winter, we desire spring. There are countless such examples: we all want to be done with whatever is going on, so we can "finally" live our lives. This takes place especially when we dislike what we go through, but it is a general attitude of dividing the world into two realms, this world and another one which we expect.

There is also another kind of expectation, the one you can experience during the pre-sanctified liturgies of the Great Lent. They silence my divided way of seeing the world and push me toward oneness. You wake up in the morning, and the first thought you have is that there is liturgy in the evening, which means that you need *to prepare*. First, you need to fast: no eating and drinking before the liturgy. A nuisance, one may say, but it is a blessing. You become present, and not because of any virtue you may have, but rather because of a desire. You wish to go to dinner in the evening,

---

1. Yannaras, *Person and Eros*, 5.

and this transforms your whole day. You no longer just pass by some fruit or some piece of bread and put it thoughtlessly in your mouth. You remember what is to come, and this makes you aware of everything you do in the present. You also remember that you cannot approach the chalice with negative thoughts toward your fellows, so you avoid fighting over petty things, getting angry at meetings, or participating in meaningless discussions. I'm not saying that you succeed in doing all these things; the point is that you are present and *think of them*.

The reason for this is an expectation. You wait for the liturgy, for the Kingdom on earth. But notice how the entire world, this world, the daily one, is transformed by this orientation; notice how, instead of making you absent, instead of making you move your mind into what may come next and thus in imagination, the wait for the hour of communion makes every little moment of your *present* life count in a completely different light. The world itself, in the weakness of your body which is hungry and thirsty, in the weakness of your mind which judges and gets angry, is transformed into the kingdom. The Kingdom that waits for you in the chalice transforms your world into a kingdom.

Fr. Arsenie Boca, as others before him, said (and I cite from memory), "We will not live after death in a different kingdom than the one we live during life."[2] If we always wait for our lives to finally begin, they may never begin. Life has already begun if it ever is to begin.

---

2. Boca, *Living Words*, 163.

Angels and Birth-givers

REGARDLESS OF WHERE I am, I always try to call my mom on March 25. It is the Annunciation, and I know she has always loved this day. I don't often have something to tell her. There is nothing spectacular in my life. However, being together in the moment, something is said. The "she and I" is being said. When calling other people, the "they and I" is being said.

Regardless of the words used, the being together is "love" in all these situations. What if I respond to it with the words of the Virgin: "Be it done unto me according to Thy word!"

The Annunciation . . . Giving yourself up in the arms of love, regardless of perils, of shame, of disgrace . . . Giving yourself up—becoming a birth-giver of that with which you are unknowingly pregnant: the Beautiful! "When the soul, when our whole being becomes pure, when we . . . attain the state of virginity . . . Jesus is born in our being."[1] Pregnant with the Beautiful we are. But we can also be birth-givers of the Beautiful.

The Annunciation reminds us of one other thing: we also need an angel to remind us of our pregnancy. Perhaps we can all be angels to one another, and doing so, without even realizing, we give birth to the beautiful in us and in others.

---

1. Boca, *Living Words*, 60.

Stories from Communism

"Before the communists took our land, our parents always punished us when we, children, took an apple from a tree on the street or cherries from a neighbor's garden," a friend, Adrian, told me once. "It was theft, and such a thing was not acceptable, even if, for us, it was just part of our life in the village, running around with our friends, playing, and picking up an apple when we were hungry."

The communists came, and people lost their lands and their orchards. "One day, we went on our former land, where we had the orchard, and we picked up some apples. We brought them home. It was the first time when our parents did not punish us. They did not say anything, but they had tears in their eyes."

During communism, at the beginning of the school year, for a month or so, middle school and high school students were sent to work on the fields to gather potatoes, apples, grapes, depending on what the land was producing in that part of the country. The government had already collectivized the land, and they needed free labor. Officially, it was called *practica agricolă*. Something like a practicum course in agriculture.

It was a period of time when you could find no produce in the grocery stores. Everything was rationed, and people were waiting in huge lines whenever they heard that some product or another (sugar, eggs, or potatoes) was "given out" at the store.

My region was a potato land, so we were taken out to gather potatoes from the field. A friend of mine, Cristi, told me one day, "I will get some potatoes, so my mom could make mashed potatoes for my brother this evening." Cristi's brother was two years old. Their dad had died, and their mother was their only support. Cristi was a very serious kid, somehow older than his age.

We were not supposed to get potatoes from the field. It was a crime, because we would steal "the potatoes of the people." The same people who had no potatoes at home.

Cristi got some potatoes in his bag that day. He chose only the smallest ones. He thought that nobody would care about it. It was probably one or two pounds. At the end of the day, we got into the bus that had to take us back into the city. After a short drive, we were stopped, and the "agents" (whoever they were) came in the bus and checked our bags. They found the small potatoes in Cristi's bag, yelled at him, took the bag out, and emptied it on the field. Nobody cared about those potatoes, but a kid should not be allowed to steal from the property "of the people."

What Would I Have Done

I HAVE OFTEN HEARD people wondering what they would have done if they lived during communism: would they have become persecutors or informants for the secret police? Would they have had the strength to say no to the temptation to save themselves at the expense of their fellow humans? The same question appears when people discuss the Holocaust or other horrific events during the history of humanity. What would I have done if I had lived during those times?

This question can easily become a way to tell ourselves that we are better than others. Few of us are able to say that we may have been an agent of the secret police, a prison guard, a torturer, or a Nazi officer. The firm belief in our moral strength does not allow us to consider this possibility. Other times, however, the question becomes torturous, because it reveals to us that the world is not so clearly divided between good and evil and because we discover that we might not have had the power to sacrifice convenience for truth. We acknowledge that we are rather weak before the "voice of reason" which tells us that we owe it to ourselves to remain alive, regardless of the means to do so. This "voice of reason" comes slowly and progressively; we are rarely in the situation in which we need to choose between pure good and evil. Instead, we perceive ourselves as human beings in connection with others and so we believe it is safe to do what others do, to show, at least, that we think like them, so they accept us and thus protect us. Actions that we consider glorious in stories may appear in a different light at such moments: they become irrational. Here are some examples. Is it rational to say that you still believe in God if this statement produces hatred in your torturer to the point where you are left in a pool of blood? Is it rational to say no to collaboration with the secret police when you are menaced with your family's suffering and when you perceive that many of your friends already do it? Is it rational to leave behind everything you have and go into the mountains to form a resistance movement and thus live as an outcast with a death sentence of your head? Is it rational to give your piece of bread to your fellow inmate when you are yourself on the brink of death through starvation?

I think many would say that it is rather folly, and we would acknowledge that the power of "reason" convinces us to be what we despise when we read stories of persecution: the torturers themselves.

Regardless of the way in which we answer this question, "What would I have done," it is rather a fruitless enterprise, leading only to separation from our own self. We disappear from the present and move into a realm that we cannot change and even less understand. We lose the possibility of being present in the world that is given to us in this moment. This is the reason why, when discussing communist persecution and the response people had in Romania between 1946 and 1989, people often have an introspection into the depth of one's soul. To think about terror is to think about how I respond to life each and every moment: by focusing on me or by giving my life to the other.

Afraid to Be in Heaven

It is quite scary to think about being in heaven. In this beautiful country I would be naked. All my dark thoughts, my evil desires, my shortcomings, in one expression, all those things that I try to keep hidden from everyone I encounter would be out in the open.

I think it would feel like finding myself naked in a public space or meeting someone without brushing my teeth in the morning, without taking a shower—all methods of cleansing me of my stinkiness.

One may say that to be able to get to heaven, I should do precisely this: cleanse myself of evil, so I can be received in such a beautiful country. I don't deny it. If I did not think I would need to clean up when I go in public, I would consider that I *deserve* to be accepted regardless of how I am. But one more thing is needed: to overcome the fear of being seen just as I am. I do not deserve to be accepted as I am, but I am already loved despite who I am.

There is one way in which those who are in heaven seem to have overcome this fear: seeing others in their nakedness, they run to take care of these people's wounds, forgetting their own putrid abscesses. Running to embrace others is equivalent with their acceptance of the Embrace.

This is probably my only hope to be in heaven: to be embraced by those who have forgotten their fear.

One may see here an explanation for why, in Orthodoxy, we pray to the saints: we ask them, who have already accepted the

Embrace, to embrace us as well, so through them we receive the power to overcome fear and accept the Embrace.

Identity Stories

STORY NUMBER ONE: A few years ago, in an American town in Indiana, I used to play soccer in a semi-competitive adult league. One of my teammates was a Mexican man, and we got along quite well. One day, he told me that I should join him and his friends for their scrimmages; they were getting together once a week for two hours of friendly soccer. They were all Mexicans, so they used Spanish during the game. They accepted me without questions and addressed me in English if necessary, although I could understand what was needed. After one hour or so, we took a break, and some of the players asked my friend in Spanish, "who is the gringo?" My friend answered, "Oh, he's no gringo. He's Romanian." "Ah, bueno, bueno!" End of discussion; we went back to soccer, and I think I received many more passes the second half.

I did not know what "gringo" meant, so I asked some friends afterwards. The decision of the majority was that "gringo" was a term used to designate white Americans. I looked white, which would place me in the "gringo" category, but I was Romanian, and this excluded me, my friends told me. The truth is that the moment they found out "I was not a gringo," they truly accepted me as one of theirs: I was a foreigner, just as they were, a foreigner coming from Europe (and, by consequence, having "football" in his blood), so I couldn't possibly be a "gringo" even if I looked like one.

Story number two: another Midwest American town, in an ethnic grocery store. A Middle Eastern woman comes into the store and speaks with the owner in Arabic. I go in line to pay, and

I smile when our eyes meet. She is quite full of life and greets me. I greet her back, and she immediately asks me a question, clearly expecting a different answer than the one I had: "Where are you from?" "Originally from Romania," I answer. A little disappointed, the lady says, "Oh, I thought you were one of ours." On that day, my exterior appearance did not say "gringo." I had not shaved for a few days, my beard had grown, and I was in a Mediterranean store. All this suggested I was from the Middle East.

I answered with the first words that came to my mouth, "What do you mean? I am one of yours!" The lady started to laugh—she saw, I believe, that, to an extent, I was one of theirs: I was a human, just like her. We continued talking until we paid for our purchases.

The online dictionary gives a very interesting account for *gringo*: from Mexican Spanish *gringo*, contemptuous word for "foreigner," from Spanish *gringo*, "foreign, unintelligible talk, gibberish," perhaps ultimately from *griego* "Greek." The "Diccionario Castellano" (1787) says gringo was used in Malaga for "anyone who spoke Spanish badly" and in Madrid for "the Irish."

There is something spectacular about "Greek" being the origin of gringo: the Greeks themselves had a word for those who could not speak their language: *barbaros*. Poor witnesses for people are the eyes and ears of those who have barbarous souls, Heraclitus says, arguably meaning that these souls cannot speak Greek. But let Heraclitus be.

Sometimes there is a very thin line between being a *gringo* and not being a *gringo*, between being a *barbaros* and not being a *barbaros*: possessing the language of soccer, a different citizenship, or a beard which had not been shaved for a few days.

Praise and the Evil Eye

After two hours in a shuttle from Chișinău to Bucharest, we took a break at a gas station. Just in front of my seat, a woman was holding her six-month-old baby in her arms. We came out of the shuttle, and my wife started speaking with this lady, complimenting the wonderful behavior of the child. "Such a nice girl!" she said. "Aren't you the best child?"

The little girl smiled at my wife and waved her hands erratically. However, the demeanor of her mom changed: "No, stop it!" she said. "Don't say that! You'll charm her, and she'll cry! No, I'm not a good girl," she started saying, as if she was the child herself. "I am bad; I am the worst; I am not good!" Then, trying to avoid being seen, she put her hand on her bottom. There is a Romanian saying: "Cum nu se deoache fundul meu, așa să nu se deoache copilul meu!" In English it would be something like this: "As my bottom is not charmed, may it be that my child is not charmed either!"

The lady was referring to the evil eye—a superstitious belief that, in large terms, says that people can cause misfortune to someone else when they look at them with envy or evil thoughts. This does not mean that the lady believed my wife was not well-intended. It was rather a more "Romanian" understanding of "evil eye." In this case, the lady was afraid that my wife's praise may take away from the child's protection, may open her to the mercy of evil forces.

Indeed, traditional cultures from the East seem to believe that pride is the root of all evil. On the one hand, praise may lead to pride. On the other hand, and this was, I think, the case with this mother and her child, wherever praise is, the devil comes as well. From the mother's point of view, the child was at the mercy of evil forces. If anyone said something good, these forces, the demons, would hear immediately and come in legions. The odd reaction of the mother had something to do with this: she did not want to attract possible evil powers.

Sure enough, when we went back into the shuttle, the child started to cry. Of course, it may have been because she had too many clothes on her (Romanians are famous for overdressing their children), as my wife and I thought. Or she may have been tired, or her teeth were coming in. But her mom did not think of any of these reasons. For her, the child was attacked. So, between her "shh, shh, shh, shh" sounds, she said from time to time, "Dear child, the Lord be with you!"

Was the child attacked by evil forces? What do I know about this? But what I know is that before we talked about it, the child was silent; once we brought this fact into the light, once we stated it and gave it a name, things were disturbed. Even if the child remained silent, things were already disturbed: we talked about it. Was there any need to do so?

Lucian Blaga, a Romanian philosopher and poet, who allegedly did not speak before he was four years old, says something like this in one of his poems: *Eu nu strivesc corola de minuni a lumii.*[1] "I do not crush the world's crown of wonders."

Perhaps we did.

---

1. Blaga, "Eu nu strivesc," 33.

The Restoration of Memory as Public Sacrament

IN THE EARLY NINETIES, just a few years after the fall of communism in Romania, a Westerner visiting Bucharest told me something that shocked me back then: "Why do all people look as if they were hit with a hammer on their heads?" I remember looking around—we were in a bus station. It was the first time that it occurred to me that people did indeed look lost. It was not just that I could meet no eyes and people had their eyes fixed into an emptiness that seemed to suck their souls, but there was also a complete lack of connection. We did not know how to connect to another, especially because we had lost the ability to connect with ourselves.

I have heard people (Ana Blandiana and Ioana Haşu come first to mind) speaking of communism as a disease because we, those who went through it, are people without memory, since the regime wanted to erase everything connecting us with the past and with our ancestors. Absolute submission can only be obtained when an individual is utterly alone, when all his or her connections within family or community disappear. In this disease, we have forgotten ourselves, our way to connect with others.

We were sick in communism, and we learned to live with this sickness to the point where it became our way of life. Some time ago, I heard someone (I think it was Fr. Thomas Hopko, but I am no longer sure) suggesting that we should consider what would happen if the prodigal son did not go back to his father's house. Fr.

Hopko, if indeed it was him, said that the prodigal may tell a story to his children, letting them know that there is a country which he had lost, a country in which there was plenty for all. Over generations, the story would be transformed into legend, and no one would take it as a memory. The only "reality" would be given by the new world in which the generations coming from the prodigal son formed their lives. They would be sick without knowing it, because they would perceive their sickness as reality. They would be people without memory.

To some extent, this happened in communism too. We lived in a sick world that many began to consider "normal," and we no longer knew how to deal with our disease. This is why public discourse about communism is needed. People who lived it, especially if they experienced trauma in their families, face the impossibility of coming back to the country of their father, which in this case means to come back to their genuine selves. The suffering buried within them, within us, does not even allow us to go back to the lost land because we forgot it is still possible. This disease brings us the impossibility of transcendence. Speaking of communism is the occasion to bring this disease to the surface. It is not about giving people a justification for their suffering, for their impossibility to return to the lost land. It is rather about acknowledging that we have this disease and about being able to recognize it in public. This does not mean that we are horrible because we are sick or that we are entitled to others' understanding; it is only the occasion to return to who we are.

Revealing this disease is the first step in a public sacrament; it is the first step in returning human nature to itself. Restoring our memory is a liturgical endeavor because it creates the occasion of giving back to the world (to us) its nature. It is one way of fulfilling our call to be priests of creation.

Some Thoughts on Levinas and Orthodoxy

IN THE ESSAY ON "Judaism and Christianity" from *In the Time of the Nations*, Emmanuel Levinas recalls a story mentioned by Hannah Arendt. When she was a child, she said one day to the rabbi, "You know, I have lost my faith." And he responded, "Who's asking you for it?'" Levinas says,

> The response was typical. What matters is not "faith," but "doing." Doing, which means moral behavior, of course, but also the performance of the ritual. Moreover, are believing and doing different things? What does believing mean? What is faith made of? Words, ideas? Convictions? What do we believe with? With the whole body! With all my bones (Psalm 35:10)! What the rabbi meant was: "Doing good is the act of belief itself." That is my conclusion.[1]

I am positive you see here the beauty of Levinas's thoughts. But I think you can also see the danger: if one perceives oneself as the source of "doing good," one already is in the pit of self-idolatry, of creating a god of himself. Certainly, one can make something bad out of anything good, and my last statement may just transform a beautiful thought into ugliness. But there remains the question of what "doing good" might mean. Some say this question belongs to the discourse of the West, the language of philosophy, which wants to give definitions to all things, to have boundaries and clarity. In

---

1. Levinas, *In the Time of the Nations*, 148.

the same essay quoted above, Bishop Hemmerle, Levinas's interlocutor, seems to search for such clarity: "I often wonder whether I am not betraying him, even when what I do seems right at the moment I am doing it."[2] Wondering whether this or that is the right thing seems to deal with a truth that can be checked, verified, which Levinas criticizes.

In fact, when I approached Levinas, I always felt that I could not recognize myself, an Orthodox Christian, in the Christianity which was sometimes put down during the discussions I had with my peers. The "scientific truth" of the Bible was never an issue for me. Whether the Bible is or is not the Truth was an incomprehensible question, for I had not applied truth and falsity to the statements in the text but rather to what was beyond the mere words. There is no sense in claiming that, on the road to Emmaus, Jesus opened Luke's and Cleopas's eyes to be able to understand Scripture unless truth is beyond statements. Truth is not thus subject to my evaluation. I cannot realize whether I betray Christ by checking whether my actions are in agreement with truth: this is what the Pharisee does, finding justification in his moral life. Asking whether I am betraying him who calls upon me to act can be the beginning of a movement in which I either blame or idolatrize myself. That is, I begin with me and not with Truth.

Eastern Orthodoxy perceives things differently. Kenosis, the emptying of oneself, is seen in the East as making space for energies that are not of oneself but rather of a radical Other. In kenosis, one becomes truth by acting as truth—by believing with all of one's bones. Perhaps this would mean taking the same road with him who calls upon my responsibility—giving yourself to the Other.

There is an icon (icons in Orthodoxy are not objects of worship but windows of the soul; they are venerated because divinity is present through these windows) where Jesus knocks at the door of a house. On the other side of the door, people busy themselves with their human lives. But there is a striking difference between the two sides of the door: on the inside, the door has a handle; on the outside, it does not. The door cannot be opened from the

---

2. Levinas, *In the Time of the Nations*, 149.

outside. The call of the Other is always there, but it is only you who can give yourself up. In order to open the door, you have to be prepared to give yourself to the Other, to the point where it is no longer you who live, but the Other lives in you. If the Other lives in you, then you can no longer perceive yourself as the source of your actions. If you are the source, then you are also object of idolatry—I am giving myself to the other and I am fully proud of it. Opening the door to Christ in Eastern Orthodoxy means allowing Christ to act in you. In other words, you become yourself an embodiment of the Torah.

Now think of this icon I just described as a text with gaps—perhaps we need a midrash to read it. Father Arsenie Boca, a Romanian priest and monk who suffered immensely during communism—people of all faiths were imprisoned simply because they did not renounce their faith—said in one of his homilies, published under the title *Living Words* (the title itself is suggestive for the way in which Orthodoxy understands texts—if these texts are of any value, it is because they are alive and, as people do, live and call upon us), that the reason why we do not open the door to Jesus, to the Other, is because we do not even find this door anymore. What we do in life is creating a God in our image; we posit things about God, we surround ourselves with beliefs, our own little gods, our mirrors, and we busy ourselves with contemplating these images, these creations, further closing us up in our own caves. In a room filled with furniture, our furniture, the door is no longer seen. Thus, the call of the Other is no longer even perceived because we answer only to the call of the one whom we take to be another when we look in mirrors. This so-called "other" that we see in mirrors is the conglomeration of beliefs that we mistakenly call the self.

I mentioned above the story of Hannah Arendt confessing her loss of faith. Allow me to tell you another story from someone's confession. A friend of mine once went to confession and summed up the courage to tell her priest that she did not like to go to church and participate in the liturgy; she preferred to do things for others. This could be taken in two ways. On the one hand, it must sound good, Levinasian—"doing good is the act of belief itself"—so the priest should have congratulated her. On the other hand, participating in liturgy, or being part of the church (the body of Christ), is an important part of being a Christian, so the lady was right to fear some scolding from the part of the priest. But he did not do any of these things. He only asked her, "What do you do for them, then?"

At that very moment, my friend started to cry. Tears during confession are welcome because they are seen as a new baptism: you are washed by the water pouring out of your own wounds. In her case, my friend's tears were her realization that the refusal to participate in tradition was itself a worship—a worship of the self. "I am above liturgy; I am above tradition; I know what is good—doing things for others." The priest's question was a mirror which revealed to her that she was not doing anything.

Perhaps Orthodoxy and Levinas's philosophy are not far away from each other. In both we find a faith of the bones, a lived faith. In the words of Father Arsenie Boca, whom I mentioned before, the Kingdom is present here, on earth, in what we do for one another. There is no life in the Kingdom of Heaven unless we already live in it here, on earth. Allow me to emphasize this: not believe in it, but live in it.

The Church and the Problem of the Third

A FRIEND OF MINE told me once that "the Orthodox Church does not have an answer to the problem of the third." His perspective was Levinasian. He believed that Orthodoxy does not have an answer regarding how to go from the relationship with one other human being to the relationship with a third, that is, from the ethical to the political. He expressed the problem in concrete terms: the church asks you to love your enemy, your persecutor; the answer from communist prisons is found precisely here, in the responsibility that the persecuted experiences for the soul of the persecutor. However, the church has nothing to say, my friend told me, to the one who could not care less about it, to the one who does not persecute the faithful but does not feel part of them either. The church does not talk about loving the indifferent.

Another friend of mine told me once that each human being is a church under reconstruction. There is beauty in each one of these churches, but when you visit them (so when you enter in communication with other people), you are so overwhelmed by the construction, by the work of restoration, that you no longer grasp the beauty hidden under this work.

The beauty hidden in each of these churches, waiting to be restored, is Christ, and Christ crucified, as Paul says. Anytime the institutional church has nothing to say to the third, that is, to the one who finds no connection with it, anytime it does not weep for the absence of communication with this third, the church may need to ask itself whether it has forgotten the real Third, Christ crucified in all and each of these small churches in restoration. For the church is the Body of Christ crucified for all these other bodies.

Anytime I have the problem of the third, not being able to love the one for whom my life is an enigma and to rejoice in his life, I am not in the church.

Laughter, Levinas, and the Otherwise than Being

LEVINAS SUGGESTS THAT THE "otherwise than being" is to be understood in being, although "it" differs absolutely from essence. It "has no genus in common with essence, and is said only in the breathlessness that pronounces the extra-ordinary word beyond. Alterity figures in it outside any qualification of the other for the ontological order and outside any attribute."[1]

What is there to understand about the otherwise than being? Here is a possibility: imagine Abraham bursting into laughter the moment he receives the commandment to kill his son, his only one, the one he loves, Isaac (Genesis 22). There are at least three possible ways to interpret this laughter:

1. Abraham becomes crazy (after all, totally understandable, given that he'll likely lose his son);
2. Abraham thinks God is crazy and laughs in the face of this creature who calls himself God;
3. Abraham is at a loss, is silent, and this silence is expressed in laughter.

There might be something in the first laughter that avoids philosophy, being. Crazy people talk but don't really say anything; at the same time, something is said. But what is said seems to be outside of our power of comprehension. Nevertheless, we

---

1. Levinas, *Otherwise than Being*, 16.

understand what is said as being otherwise than normal discourse, as not being something. If this is so, then maybe we should call this laughter the laughter of the non-being.

However, the laughter of the insane, as much as it may not be placed within the being defined by others, is still some being; we can make it familiar. It does not escape philosophy.

Can Abraham's second kind of laughter escape being? Abraham thinks God has lost his mind and laughs in the face of this creature who calls himself God. This kind of laughter seems to be close to Kundera's devilish laughter, or even to Socratic irony. Realizing he has engaged in some kind of rituals that became his God, having believed in a God that no longer makes any sense, Abraham laughs. He laughs and rejects everything that proposes itself as a possible solution to how to live his life. This laughter comes with a feeling of non-belongingness and falling out of the realm of the others. Kundera says in his *The Book of Laughter and Forgetting*:

> I wandered through the streets of Prague, rings of laughing, dancing Czechs swirled around me, and I knew that I did not belong to them but belonged to Kalandra, who had also come loose from the circular trajectory and had fallen, fallen, to end his fall in a condemned man's coffin, but even though I did not belong to them, I nonetheless watched the dancing with envy and yearning, unable to take my eyes off them.[2]

Kundera has lost something that was familiar to him, has lost what he used to call being, but he remains in a place that is determined by something that is not present, which he experiences as a loss. Since the place where he is lacks something that is, something defined by ontology, this place too is part of ontology. We can imagine Abraham himself yearning for the faith he enjoyed having, for the assurance that belonging to the circle gave him. Now, laughing at all the nonsense around him, he does not find anything to grasp. In a way, he even lost his son Isaac, the laughter and the promise that God gave him: there would be a great nation coming from his

---

2. Kundera, *Book of Laughter*, 93–94.

seed. But this sense of a loss is powerful and brings fear. Rejecting everything, one like Abraham finds oneself in a space where the only thing present is the fear of death.

Bringing in the presence of death, this laughter might be what we are looking for; death itself seems to be beyond being. But death is part of being precisely by being non-being: the not-being partakes of being, as the Stranger says in *The Sophist*. This is still not the laughter for which we are searching. In fact, the devilish laughter, while rejecting all possible theories, all possible circles, becomes itself a circle, a theory.

Socratic irony is also a laughter in the face of a god—our opinions, our truths. As Bakhtin says in "Epic and Novel" in *The Dialogic Imagination: Four Essays by M. M. Bakhtin*, "It is precisely laughter that destroys the epic, and in general destroys any hierarchical (distancing and valorized) distance."[3] Socratic laughter seems to have a cleansing function: it rejects all opinions that one has.

But there are dangers. On the one hand, this space of freedom, of inconclusiveness, can become the new king. "I only know I don't know anything, and I am proud of it." "I only know that I do not know anything" has the problem of still knowing something, perhaps that there is nothing to know. In other words, you laugh at everything, and your laughter becomes your ideology. So this option still leaves us with the question whether there is any possibility to refuse idolatry without becoming idolatrous. Or, in other words, whether there is any possibility for a genuine moral ethical attitude, one that would avoid any ideology.

On the other hand, the second danger comes from the nothingness that the ironic laughter produces. Surrounded by the nothingness he created around him by laughing in the face of God, Abraham becomes indeed insane or feels he is dead. He is outside the circle, as Kundera puts it, but he is still craving one.

We remain at a loss. It might be that, as Vladimir and Estragon in *Waiting for Godot*, we find out that there is nowhere to go. But what if we do not try to go anywhere? What if the third kind of laughter takes place when Abraham is at a loss, silent, a

---

3. Bakhtin, *Dialogic Imagination*, 23.

silence that is laughter and is not laughter at the same time, is the thing beyond any comprehension but which is the genuine understanding itself? An attitude that does not have cause and does not present itself as a cause of something else. An attitude that we cannot say that it is, an attitude that cannot be included in our categories of being and non-being. An attitude purely and simply other. An attitude that cannot be named and about which we talk only saying that it is like . . . like laughter, or maybe like silence. Or maybe like responsibility. But it is neither of them really.

There is no solution to Abraham's dilemma; even the "no solution" is not a solution. If we see this "solution" as a solution, as an answer to a problem, then we fall again from one circle to another. We might say that this circle is superior because it understands the difficulties of the first one, where we were still looking for solutions. There are people who live in a circle, and there are people who live in a circle and realize it, being aware that they cannot escape it. The latter seem superior. But this second circle is still not superior because, as the previous one, it still does not see its own problems. We would still be imitations of Vladimir and Estragon, maybe more aware that there is nothing to be done, but still trapped within the play of waiting for something.

In the face of the incomprehensible commandment, Abraham laughs. Or he suspends judgment—he becomes silent. His laughter itself is a way of not saying anything. It is not that he makes a conscientious decision in the face of the evidence that there is no decision to be made, whether he must kill his son or not. If laughter is a choice, then laughter becomes idolatrous. Abraham's laughter is the realization that no judgment can be made and not the result of that. Laughter, or silence, for there is no difference between the two now, is the activity in which Abraham engages when he realizes that the kind of knowledge required from him is too powerful to be known, is a knowledge that shatters the individual and takes him out of his world. God's command to Abraham throws him in darkness expressed in laughter. But in this darkness, something else appears: "There is no judgment." Abraham knows that he cannot say that he must not offer his son as an offering-up and that he cannot say that he must kill his son. And he laughs. His laughter now cannot follow a decision. If it were a decision, then it would be nothing else than an idolatrous movement, one that replaces an idolatrous love—as long as love for anything other than God, so love for the son who ensures that his seed will give birth to a mighty nation is idolatrous—with another idolatrous love. Abraham does not start climbing up Mount Moriah after taking the decision to obey God's command to sacrifice Isaac. The Abraham of this third laughter cannot decide to obey any command. He does not decide to do anything—he just presents himself, "here I am," and the decision is already comprised in this attitude. His action is determined by the genuinely ethical attitude of presenting oneself as the first and most responsible individual. If Abraham says that God will see to the offering-up, he expresses his genuine attitude of trusting his fate in the hands of God. The absence of any kind of judgment is the apparition of what Levinas calls responsibility. Or maybe it is the attitude of giving death to oneself, as Derrida might call it, or loving one's life so much as to be able to renounce it.

This death resides in the incomprehensibility itself—things can no longer have logos and thus cannot participate into being. In this incomprehensibility Abraham holds nothing, not even incomprehensibility itself, for it cannot be held. This other death is the laughter beyond life and death, beyond day and night, beyond being and non-being. It is the realization that being cannot be but intertwined with non-being, that any authentic belief cannot be but embodied with ideology, and this realization becomes laughter. Or silence.

The third kind of laughter opens the possibility of acting ethically—it orients us differently in life. We could say that laughter in general helps us to avoid making any totaling claim. This is especially the case for Socratic irony. But this kind of laughter opens the possibility of the third kind, which is not an answer to anything but rather is the only thing one can do the moment one is about to see the Good beyond being. It is the only thing that one can do in the sense that one cannot not do it.

Nothing to Be Done: Waiting for Godot

THE OPENING LINE OF Beckett's *Waiting for Godot*, "nothing to be done," seems to be rather a closure. If there is nothing to be done, then maybe we should indeed do nothing. Or, better, not even nothing should count for something to be done. Here we have what our age has been looking for: a final answer—there is no answer. It might be too easy, though, to say that *Waiting for Godot*, or, for that matter, any text suggesting that there are no answers and that we try too much to find meaning where there is none, fails in contradictions. After all, this problem seems to be as old as Western thought, since maybe Socrates's "I only know that I don't know anything." We know that there is no conclusion, and instead of liberating ourselves from the power of any definition, we remain determined by our new god: "there is no god." In this sense, "nothing to be done" still leaves us in a realm where, while it seems that we liberated ourselves from all prejudices and preconceptions of truth, "nothing to be done" becomes the new norm, the new language, the new philosophy.

But then, at the end of the play, Estragon asks, "And if we dropped him?"

The question cannot, after all, have an answer. If we dropped Godot for good, would we be able to leave this place? It seems it depends on what we mean by "dropping." In a sense, leaving this place, this "here," is never possible, for we would always arrive still "here." It would be a different "here," a here that is not-here, if we think about the first here, but still a here. We leave behind a theory, an idol, by falling into another one.

> Vladimir: Well? Shall we go?
> Estragon: Yes, let's go.
> They do not move.[1]

Imagine Vladimir and Estragon bursting in laughter and falling into each other's arms ...

They have already left.

---

1. Beckett, *Waiting for Godot*, 109.

We Are All to Blame

"We're all to blame, all of us . . . if only everyone could be convinced of that . . ."[1]

These words are uttered by Shatov, a character in Dostoevsky's *Devils*. The idea that we are all responsible for the sins of others is not a novelty in Dostoevsky's works. It appears in *Crime and Punishment*, published before the *Devils*, and especially in *The Karamazov Brothers*, where several characters utter it in different ways. For example, Mitya, the eldest or the Karamazov brothers, says, "We are all cruel, we are all monsters, we all cause suffering to people . . . but . . . I'm worse than anyone."[2]

One of the prayers before the Eucharist reveals the same idea: "I believe, O Lord, and I confess that You are truly the Christ, the Son of the Living God, Who came into the world to save sinners, of whom I am first." The prayer is said by all people participating in the liturgy together, just before approaching the chalice.

Such words, including Shatov's, bring forth the idea that we all have responsibility for the suffering of others. However, if Zosima's and Mitya's words seem to emphasize the responsibility that one accepts—a responsibility that precedes him—Shatov's expression has a different flavor: "If only everyone could be convinced of that . . ."

Shatov utters these words after he finds out that his wife, whom he hasn't seen in three years, is pregnant and is about to

---

1. Dostoevsky, *Devils*, 656.
2. Dostoevsky, *Karamazov Brothers*, 641.

deliver a baby. With no questions, no judgments, no accusations, he runs to find a midwife. In a moment when he could have felt that he had been wronged, he says, "We're all to blame, all of us..."[3] It is, I take it, a description of the human condition: we are born into this world, we participate in it, and so we must acknowledge that its scars are manifestations of our own behaviors.

Still, in the midst of this pure feeling, Shatov says, "If only everyone could be convinced of that..."

This is such a human reaction, and, at the same time, the seed of our judgment for our brethren... The desire to have others see that they are just like you, responsible for their and your suffering, is one of the most understandable desires one could have, be it in interpersonal relationships or in society.

You feel your spouse has harmed you, and your suffering may blind you at first. But then you may still realize that you are to be blamed, for in this world of sinners "I am the first." You see her absence as manifestation of your own lack of presence, of your own inadequacy, and so your perceived suffering is transformed in love. Still, a thought creeps into your heart: "If only she could be convinced that she also is to blame..." And this is not because you consider that she has any guilt but rather because we are all made from the same mud, we live in the same world, and thus we are touched by all of its impurities. This little thought brings your defeat... For you no longer say, "I am the first sinner, I am first responsible for all" but rather that she is the first one, even if you don't realize you are saying it.

When the third comes in, and so the political, Shatov's words become even more dangerous. "If only everyone could see how they are responsible for the lives of the others..." Of course, I am responsible as well, but they must see it too. They must see that this world depends on them. There is one step from the beauty of Shatov's words to ugliness and death. These words are the creed of any totalitarian society, which comes to claim that we are all responsible and equal in that responsibility. And those who do not

---

3. Dostoevsky, *Devils*, 656.

see it are "enemies of the people," individuals who must be eliminated, sent to Siberia or executed in dungeons.

"We're all to blame, all of us . . . if only everyone could be convinced of that . . ." Of course, if everyone could be convinced of that, then there would be no suffering. Shatov may not have to face a group of people dedicated to causes. Still, even so, Shatov's words invite us to vigilance against our own hearts: the demons never leave us alone, even in moments of beauty.

I Am a Nobody for Whom Someone Is on a Cross

WHEN I WAS A child, my aunt took me one day to a monastery close to where I lived: the monastery at Sâmbăta de Sus, Romania. A blind monk lived there, Father Teofil; he had fame among people. Some were saying that he had clairvoyance and he sensed people's characters, seeing what they have done. This made me afraid. I was a child, but there was something about which I was ashamed. I do not remember what it was; I just know that I did not want my parents to find out. I went to the monastery wondering how much this monk would see through me. Of course, I did not confess my fear to my aunt (why would a good Christian boy be afraid of going to a monk?), but the ride was quite uncomfortable. Father Teofil was sitting on a chair outside the small church. My aunt told him something, and then I saw him opening his arms largely, calling for me. I went towards him slowly, without opening my arms but rather keeping them close to my body, as any shy boy would do. When I reached him, he held me strongly close to his chest. I quite remember the feeling: it hurt. I don't remember what he said to me, and I don't remember whether I said anything back, but I strongly remember the feeling of being held in his arms. I could not resist, so I melted down, and then it hurt no more.

After that moment, I always longed to see Father Teofil. Whenever I met him, he looked like a joyful grandpa, ready to have a good laugh. Have you actually noticed how grandparents embrace their grandchildren? They open their arms largely and wait in that position until the child comes to them and embraces them back. Their open arms are the image of a gift—their own surrendering to the child. But it is an active and joyful surrender which is seen in the opening of their hands in the form of a cross. The grandparents wait like that on a cross until the child runs to them and embraces them back.

When we embrace people, if we do it genuinely, without any restraints, we open our arms largely, as if we were on a cross. Any genuine embrace begins on a cross, in giving ourselves to the other. And perhaps our lack of ability to embrace others may just be the reason Christ still is on the cross. He waits for us to embrace Him back, and so He remains with His arms open to embrace the whole of humanity. It is a gift of love that does not depend on our response. What depends on us is His descent: our embracing Him back would make His hands come round us.

If we are made in the image and likeness of God, then each one of us is made to be on the cross for the other. We were made to be our brothers' keepers. We were made to be on the cross for our brothers. But the being together of these brothers ("How good it is for brothers to be together"—Psalm 133) brings all crosses in a universal embrace. Christ waits for me on the cross in every person I encounter. Whenever I judge and so refuse the other, I refuse to take Him down from the cross. Regardless of how buried He is in him or her, He waits for my embrace so He can come down.

The path toward Christ goes through the other, any other I encounter. I cannot embrace Christ alone. Who am I to ask Him to come down only for me? He cannot embrace me at the expense of the world or at the expense of any other human being. He needs to remain on the cross for them. If I truly want to take down Christ from the cross, I need to bring the entire world to Him in me. This means I cannot embrace Him unless I am also on the cross, for each and every one of my neighbors.

I am a nobody for whom Christ is on the cross. And I am a mighty nobody, for I have the power to bring Him down from the cross. May I have the weakness to accept it.

The Pigs Who "Took" the Light

IF YOU LIVED IN Romania during communism, you probably remember the beautiful evenings in which an entire family gathered around the light of a candle or a gas lamp. Ceausescu, the dictator of the country, planned to pay the entire external debt, so he imposed a harsh austerity on the population. Electricity was often "taken" in the evenings, so people had to manage however they could.

Mama-mare, my grandma, was always the most vocal. Whenever we lost electricity, she used to say, "The pigs took the light again!" They had taken the "light" many times before: they took people's land, their freedom, and even their lives. *Mama-mare* was old enough to feel free to say something bad about them from time to time, but she never explained to us, the children, what she meant. When we had blackouts (at least a couple of times per week), we all just gathered in the kitchen and did whatever we could. My parents were working on their papers, *mama-mare* was cooking, and the children were doing their homework, if they were old enough, or playing.

One day, we visited someone in a village. Our host took us kids into the barn to see the animals. My brother was around three years old. When he saw the pigs, he got very excited, pointed to them and said: "They took the light last night!" Everyone smiled, but no one said anything. We all knew that *mama-mare*'s "pigs" had ears everywhere.

Losing Yourself in the Depths of Your Being

I HAVE COME TO learn that every moment of this life is an occasion to look deeper into your soul. Every such moment is also a failure, since you hardly achieve arriving there, unless, perhaps, you go through moments when everything is taken from you. Perhaps, then, it is improper to say that I have come to *learn* this, since every moment is also an occasion to realize that I haven't really learned it. Still, it is an occasion to look deeper within you because the usual temptation is to go precisely in the opposite direction: to see how the other and the world itself treat you.

I'm sure you see how funny this is: you cannot look at the other or the world unless you first see "you"; that is, you have given yourself a definition, without even acknowledging it. There is no point in saying that others mistreat you and act toward you with lack of love, respect, or fairness if you don't begin with YOU, about which you have no idea, since it is still this conceptual you that beholds yourself. Neither the "you" that you take yourself to be in looking at "you," nor the "you" at which "you" are looking is genuinely you. You live every day at the crossroad of two "forces." One of them annihilates you by, paradoxically, giving you the impression that you are something, and this force can be manifested as attack on others or even attack on yourself, two faces of the same coin. The other pulls you away from the double-headed force described above, leaving you in what seems to be a state of inaction, let's say a "force" that annihilates all forces.

I think we normally refer only to the first force, having the impression that we talk about two different things. We acknowledge that we come in contact with others and the world, and we say that we either focus on what others do to us, or we could focus on how we react before the world and learn something about it from our reaction. In this framework, we could say, for example, that you should describe how others' actions make you *feel* instead of focusing on what others do. But if we remain here, in this dichotomy, we lose ourselves. This is because this approach leaves you in the same darkness, it creates separation between you and the other, and, primarily, it separates you from yourself, leaving you in the same space of double measure in which events gain or lose in importance depending on how you are emotionally connected with the one who tells you something or with the kind of activity in which you are engaged. This force that is so much worshiped by today's world fixes you before yourself, so you no longer get lost within your depths but you disappear; in your place, your image has a dialogue with your image in the mirror.

Self-learning goes beyond this dichotomy, judging the other and falsely judging yourself. It is rather an acknowledgement that you are to always find yourself in one of these previous two situations. Discovering yourself means looking at you looking at yourself in the mirror and being surprised by your heart's movement, your patterns of thought and behavior, and your inability to avoid them even while you behold them.

In such moments you no longer see problems in others but only suffering, realizing that this suffering is a manifestation of your own disease (a disease which I would describe as your image looking at the image in the mirror).

It sounds as if you're doomed if you get there: you are no longer able to defend yourself and your feelings, you are no longer able to tell people how their actions make you feel, and so you no longer achieve "justice." Actually, this is a normal and, dare I say, desirable consequence: who cares of justice if it is not me who receives it but the "me" who beholds the "me" in the mirror?

If you truly lose yourself in the depths of your being, justice is irrelevant, because you are already free.

Short philosophical plug: this is what Socrates must think when, waiting for his execution in prison, he is *calm* and rejects Crito's attempt to free him by also rejecting justice as "giving to the other that which he deserves" ("benefit your friends and harm your enemies"). And this is why he must have said in the same context that "the good man cannot be harmed." Perhaps the good man came out of the mirror dichotomy. How can you "free" Socrates when he's already free?

Pregnant with the Beautiful

IN *BEYOND TORTURE*, A documentary about the Pitesti Phenomenon—the experiment that took place in communist prisons in Romania and that had as purpose the complete change of a human soul—Father Roman Braga recounts that he experienced the devil in Pitesti, but he found God in solitary confinement. The communists believed, he says, that if they put intellectuals in solitary confinement, these people would not resist because they need books. But the inmates discovered there themselves, and by discovering themselves they found God.

One may wonder how God is found in solitude, when Jesus Himself gives the commandment to love one's neighbor. Is it that we find God when we close ourselves to the other, when we are no longer bothered by the desires and the lack of probability that the presence of another free person brings into our lives?

It is in the answer to this question that we also find how spiritual life has meaning for "everyday" Christian living. Within ourselves, in introspection, what we find is a kingdom—and so the neighbor is there also. When you discover God within, you discover a Kingdom. But this means that I am pregnant with Beauty, with the Kingdom itself, and that the only way in which I can live with responsibility toward my nature—that of being pregnant with the Beautiful or being a birth-giver of Beauty—is to be responsible for what is in me, the God according to grace who can have life only as long as it is connected to the Kingdom.

The metaphor of pregnancy can well explain the spiritual described in Metropolitan Philip's *Meeting the Incarnate God*. We must begin with violence, he says: "The person of faith must do violence to his own heart if he will become faithful to God and his fellow."[1] In pregnancy, we must do a similar violence to our own soul if we are to be faithful to the beautiful within us. In pregnancy, we discover that we no longer belong to ourselves but to that to which we give birth. It is the first acknowledgement without which no one is called to self-violence. For we love ourselves—we love our habits, our coffee in the morning, our going to the gym. But once we are pregnant, we realize that our whole world changes. Our bodies go through events that we do not bring upon us but to which we cannot say no, unless we say no to what has a life within our body. There may be moments of despair, moments when we cry, "I want my body back," "I want my time back," or "I want my freedom back." But all these moments disappear when we hear again deep within us the call of the Beautiful, our child that is ours but is also not ours, in a deeper and more profound sense. This call of the Beautiful brings upon us responsibility toward what precedes us; this call does not allow us to say "yes" to all our desires but gives us the power to do violence to them. And we accept the pain experienced by the body with a new and surprising feeling of joy, and we are ready to embrace our new situation, that of a birth-giver of Beauty, who has the potential to give birth but is not yet there. Slowly, we open our arms to receive this Beautiful, to offer ourselves to it, and without even realizing we take upon our shoulders our cross—our own personal cross but also Christ's cross, for it is the Beautiful, the Kingdom, which awaits to take life within us. It is by this daily "violence" that takes place in carrying our cross that we express our desire to fulfill what we are called to be: birth-givers of beauty.

In this way we are co-creators of the beauty of our world. The world is already made beautiful for us, but it is such only with our activity in it, in our synergic working with God.

1. Philip and Allen, *Meeting the Incarnate God*, 55.

I mentioned above that this Beautiful with which we are pregnant is not solely of our creation. We are impregnated—we are given a gift. It is the image and likeness of God that we also find in the other. After all, this gift is the life of another. As in any relationship with other free persons, the gift is not determined and is not deserved. The gift is not limited (it has no determinations), and we have done nothing for it. But by accepting it as gift (so with no determinations and without believing that we deserve it), "we accept the condition of allowing that other entrance into our lives, allow the other to penetrate, to engage our existence through his offered gift."[2] Perhaps this is why marriage is a possible path to finding yourself: it reminds you that you cannot be in control; you depend on another free person, and you can rejoice in the other person only by enjoying her freedom. Finding yourself you find the other, who is already in you, in the Kingdom. For before you realize that you depend on others to be you, you cannot have genuine relations with other persons, but only with what you make out of them. In order to find others, to be with the others, you need to go within your depths, and from there to cry out, "I am with you."

Fr. Roman Braga said that we find ourselves within us. It does not mean that we close the door to the others. In fact, it is by closing the door to ourselves and thus going within our depths that we truly find the others: the members of the Kingdom.

---

2. Philip and Allen, *Meeting the Incarnate God*, 29.

Radical Diversity and C. S. Lewis

IN HIS WONDERFUL INTRODUCTION to St. Athanasius' *On the Incarnation*, C. S. Lewis says something that we often forget in our discussions about diversity: read old books, because these writers are much more diverse in thinking than any of our contemporary opponents.

> Every age has its own outlook. It is especially good at seeing certain truths and specially liable to make certain mistakes. We all, therefore, need the books that will correct the characteristic mistakes of our own period. And that means old books. All contemporary writers share to some extent the contemporary outlook—even those, like myself, who seem most opposed to it. Nothing strikes me more when I read the controversies of past ages than the fact that both sides were usually assuming without question a good deal which we should now absolutely deny. They thought that they were completely opposed as two sides could be, but in fact they were all the time secretly united—united with each other and against earlier and later ages—by a great mass of common assumptions. We may be sure that the characteristic blindness of the twentieth century—the blindness about which posterity will ask, 'But how could they have thought that?'—lies where we have never suspected it, and concerns something about which there is untroubled agreement between Hitler and President Roosevelt, or between Mr. H. G. Wells and Karl Barth. None of us can fully escape this blindness, but we shall certainly increase it, and weaken our

guard against it, if we read only modern books. Where they are true they will give us truths which we half knew already. Where they are false they will aggravate the error with which we are already dangerously ill. The only palliative is to keep the clean sea breeze of the centuries blowing through our minds, and this can be done only by reading old books. Not, of course, that there is any magic about the past. People were no cleverer then than they are now; they made as many mistakes as we. But not the same mistakes. They will not flatter us in the errors we are already committing; and their own errors, being now open and palpable, will not endanger us. Two heads are better than one, not because either is infallible, but because they are unlikely to go wrong in the same direction. To be sure, the books of the future would be just as good a corrective as the books of the past, but unfortunately we cannot get at them.[1]

Whenever I read this passage, I feel as someone reminds me to be humble, especially if I think I am right about something. This takes place often. Humanity tends to think in binary terms: before and after death, good and bad people, us and them.

In fact, we no longer know how to think except in binary terms. If you are a capitalist, you must be against socialism. If you are not a capitalist, then you must be a socialist. If you're not a Democrat, you must be a Republican, and if you're not a Republican, then you must be a Democrat.

How can you keep yourself from falling into categories in this life? Of course, you can read the ancients and challenge your views (and, implicitly, your age's view) with their own, but then you return here, in this reality, and anytime you open your mouth people will place you into one category or another. Regardless of how you may be and what you may think, people will always use it and place it into the categories that they understand: the categories that form their reality. Since you utter something, you are already part of their world, and so they must make sense of your account

---

1. Lewis, "Preface," 12–13.

and place it in whatever category is appropriate, in their mind, for your thought.

One possible way to react to categorization is to respond by making all sorts of distinctions: "this is not what I said," and "it is rather this than this." But anytime such attempts are done, others still will reshape you into something that you're not, burying you into the dark forest of a sophist, as Plato warned us. This is just because we, people, cannot handle what we do not understand, and we transform what we don't understand into something perceivable to us.

This does not take away my responsibility. I do not claim only the others do this, and I am absolved of my contribution to the world. After all, I already participate in it—"in sins my mother conceived me," as Psalm 50 says—and so my own body manifests its problems. C. S. Lewis's call is one to radical diversity: read the ancients. Read also the medievalists, and even the moderns. And especially read C. S. Lewis. These lectures may bring us back to a state of wonder, such as described in these verses by Lucian Blaga, Romanian poet and philosopher of the twentieth century:

> Eu nu strivesc corola de minuni a lumii
> și nu ucid
> cu mintea tainele, ce le-ntâlnesc
> în calea mea
> în flori, în ochi, pe buze ori morminte.[2]
>
> I do not crush the world's crown of wonders
> and I do not kill
> with my mind, the mysteries that I encounter
> on my way,
> in flowers, in eyes, on lips, or on sepulchers.

---

2. Blaga, "Eu nu strivesc," 33.

The Spring of Love

"Naked I came from my mother's womb, and naked I shall return to the earth. The Lord gave, and the Lord has taken away. Blessed be the name of the Lord!"[1]

Forgive me, my brothers, for crying when I say these words, Fr. Zosima says in Dostoevsky's *The Karamazov Brothers*, but they take me back to my childhood.

And I remember the small church in the cemetery, in Făgăraș . . . the great Lent, and many children sitting down in the church, listening to Fr. Aurel . . . and incense.

But Job is naked, his children died, and he lost all things.

"The Lord gave, and the Lord has taken away. Blessed be the name of the Lord!"

"Only evil contradicts good, but not the other way around," Constantin Noica says in his *Becoming Within Being*.[2]

"One can love a man only when he's out of sight; as soon as he shows his face, that's the end of love."[3] How can we love a naked face from the "dressed" perspective of our being? The face troubles us, takes us out of our comfort; it tells us to do things we don't want

---

1. Job 1:21.
2. Noica, *Becoming Within Being*, 10.
3. Dostoevsky, *Karamazov Brothers*, 297.

to do. And we don't want to do them because we are not naked but dressed in the "clothing" that we have made for ourselves.

She passes by me, and I smile to her. She smiles back. We're in an airport. Our eyes lock for a moment, they dwell within each other, and I feel so alive. An old woman, with fragile steps, but so present in the void of these full airports.

She reminds me of the *Lady in No. 6*;[4] I have no idea about the life of this old woman, but she lives in me and I in her. The Kingdom is at hand.

---

4. *The Lady in No. 6: Music Saved My Life*, a documentary directed by Malcolm Clarke on the life of the oldest Holocaust survivor.

The Temptation to Change the Suffering of the World

THERE IS ONE ASPECT of human life that we cannot change: death. In a world of uncertainty, one thing is certain: there will be a time when we will no longer be here. Before that time, there are many aspects of human life that we feel we can change, and one such aspect is as universal as death is: suffering. All of us have experienced suffering and have desired, at one moment or another, to do something about it, to act in a way that would eradicate or, at least, diminish it. This is especially the case when we see people dear to us go through terrible psychological or physical pain.

We can call this desire to eliminate suffering a desire to beautify the world. Exhausted by the ugliness that surrounds us, by innumerable instances of violence, treason, or boorishness, we want to change our reality and the people belonging to it in the name of the good. It is a simple desire to improve our world.

This is how many murderers begin, with good intentions. We've heard that "the road to hell is paved with good intentions." We know that the communists, for example, have justified torture, deportations, and killings by claiming that they eliminate the bad elements of society and that suffering of some is justified by the subsequent creation of a perfect society. But saying that we should avoid changing the world so we do not fall prey to that against which we fight is not sufficient. Speaking against the attempt to beautify the world by changing your surroundings and the people around you seems to sound like a call to passivity. However, the temptation to change the ugliness around you and to "repair" those people you believe are repairable is, in my experience at least, one of the most powerful forces of existence.

But I am not talking about a passivity that is opposed to action. In fact, I believe that this temptation to act, to do something about the ugliness of the world, can stem only from passivity, from a state in which I don't do anything for it, from a state of complacency in which I have allowed myself to forget about ugliness and to forget that it is somehow manifested in me as well, for I am part of this world.

It all begins with the self, with the focus I have on the self. I can look at the world as if it were a nice soup that I am having for dinner. I taste it, and I make a judgment: it is too salty, too sour, or too sweet. The temptation to "repair" it comes only from the position of an objective outsider. But there is another way of looking at the world. In this other way, I realize that the taste of this soup is the way it is because I am also part of it. Thus, I realize that I cannot taste it without, at the same time, tasting of myself. This realization takes place beyond the choice between passivity and action. Passivity and action are relevant when I judge something from the outside and try to decide what to do about it or whether I should do anything. I can feel "responsible" for the world, or I can believe that the only responsibility I have is for my life only. If I see myself as part of the soup, my responsibility is not a choice, but it is a way of being, and it precedes me, and it also precedes any choice I have. And so I need to work on my "taste," trusting that somehow all the other vegetables and seasons and ingredients of this soup will be touched by it. Only then will the taste of the soup be heavenly. This is the only kind of healing responsibility I can imagine.

Healing Responsibility

"I DO NOT UNDERSTAND why people talk about the past: who hurt you, why they hurt you, what kind of guilt they may have, or how you feel about it. All this does not matter; what matters is what you do now. If my child is sick, I am not worried about whether it was right for him to get sick but rather what I have to do to make him better."

I no longer remember who said this to me—it may have been during a confession. It suggests a state of presence. If I am to fully respond to what is given to me now, I cannot be also attached to why I am where I am and why the other is where he or she is.

However, should not the torturer face justice? Should not the torturer go to prison for the crimes he has committed? If we answer from the same perspective of the lines above, the answer cannot be either yes or no. Rather, the question itself is not to be asked. Of course, society should ask it and give an answer to it. But it is not a question that I, a person, can ask.

The brother of the prodigal son is upset when their father rejoices in the return of his younger son. The older brother believes that it is unjust to not make him suffer; it is not just to celebrate with the fattened calf and put a ring on his finger and a robe on him. The older brother is a man of the past. And I think that many of us, at a moment or other in this life, feel like the older son.

I recently read of a monk, Fr. Evghenie Hulea, who was imprisoned by the communists when they took power in Romania. Fr. Hulea was sent to the Canal, a labor camp, where many intellectuals, priests, peasants, or students lost their lives. Being a monk brought upon him mocking and tortures. Still, anytime he was mocked, he answered with an open heart, "God bless you, my child!"

Fr. Hulea's forgiveness is the kind that the father of the prodigal son has. It does not matter where the son was, what he did, and why he came back. He now faces him, and if he does, the father is responsible for the son's well-being. Not a moral responsibility but a healing one, which stems out of love. The prodigal son may leave again. He may take the robe and the ring, sell them, and drink the money with his friends, mocking the weakness of the father who killed the fattened calf without even thinking. Still, the father, who is always present, will have the same answer if the son ever comes back (and even if he does not): "God bless you, my child!"

Mercy and Pity

THE PRIMARY DIFFERENCE BETWEEN pity and mercy is the source of each.

In pity, it is I who have pity on another. Thus, I situate myself above him, judging him and his situation, and so taking from him human agency and even human dignity.

In mercy, the source is God. I remain on the same level with the one on whom I have mercy. I acknowledge that both of us are under the mightiness of the Creator, and I have mercy on him who is my brother because he is made of the same human flesh I am made of.

Pity stems from a world of separation, in which I detach myself from the other, see him outside of me, and even rejoice that I am not him. The pharisee has pity: "God, I thank you that I am not like other people—robbers, evildoers, adulterers—or even like this tax collector" (Luke 18:11). Someone who has pity doesn't see people but categories to which people belong.

Mercy stems from perceiving the other's wounds as manifestations of my sins and thus from being ready to be with him in his pain and sorrow. Someone who has mercy sees the person suffering beneath wounds.

Have mercy on me in my pity.

The Two Old Men

THERE IS A SHORT story of Leo Tolstoy that is predictable and moralistic at the same time: "The Two Old Men." Two old friends decide to go to Jerusalem. From the first lines of the story, you know that one behaves righteously, while the other is in need of a lesson. The story reads like a Sunday school lesson and ends in a moral statement: "And now he understood that God has commanded each of us to keep our vows in this world, so long as we live, by loving others and doing them good."[1] If it were not written by Tolstoy, the story would have been forgotten in the ocean of poor writing.

Nevertheless, there's one passage in it that redeems it; perhaps it is the way geniuses work: they plant jewels even behind poorly assembled intent.

The story goes this way. Elisei and Efim decide to go together to Jerusalem on a pilgrimage. They leave together, but they get separated for a moment, when Elisei stops in a poor village to get some water. The people in the house are sick and close to their death, which makes Elisei remain with them to help them. He responds openly and genuinely to all the needs he perceives, but doing so makes him spend much of his money, so he is no longer able to continue his journey. After the family seems to get better, Elisei returns home. Efim, after waiting for Elisei for some time, continues his journey and finally arrives in Jerusalem. His pilgrimage, though, seems to be to no benefit. Another pilgrim tells Efim

---

1. Tolstoy, "Two Old Men," 23.

that his purse was lost, and this produces in Efim "sinful thoughts." He either judges that the pilgrim lied, so the pilgrim could benefit from the goodness of the others, or he is afraid that someone may steal his own purse. Three times, Efim sees Elisei in Jerusalem, at Christ's tomb, always in front and always in a divine light. He's never able to reach him, although he tries to do so. Finally, Efim returns home, where his family seems to be in disarray and where he finally understands that "going to Jerusalem" is actually "loving others and doing them good."

In the midst of all of these predictable events, one little moment of good literature appears. Efim is on his way back home, and he happens upon the house where Elisei had stayed and where all people seem to have improved: the grandmother, the two parents, and the two children. Nothing surprising for the story so far, perhaps even too predictable, like in a bad Hollywood movie: Efim had to arrive at that house, so readers knew the outcome of Elisei's good deeds. But then Tolstoy gives details of the conversation. The grandma remembers how the stranger, "as soon as he saw us, took off his bag and put it down right here and untied it."

Notice the detail: he put the bag down right here.

The little girl joins in and says, "No, grandma, first he put his bag down on the floor in the middle of the hut, but then he put it up on the bench."[2]

Two different accounts of a most extraordinary event, one so extraordinary that you would rather consider it a fantasy. For who would think that a stranger who is on a mission, to visit Jerusalem, would stop and spend his travel money to help some dying people? If this story was cited as evidence in a court of law, jurors would be entitled to say that witnesses are not trustworthy as long as they cannot agree on small details.

And Tolstoy continues: "And the people began arguing and remembering everything he had said and done; and where he had sat, and where he had slept, and what he had done, and what he had said to them."[3]

    2. Tolstoy, "Two Old Men," 21.
    3. Tolstoy, "Two Old Men," 21.

They remembered all of this arguing, not being able to reach an agreement about how things really took place. But this is precisely the beauty of it: the truth of the events doesn't consist in the event itself but in the Truth that was poured into their lives. Through love, they were given life, and so they were able to argue about what really happened. And even if they quarrel about it, they all quarrel from within it. If you look at the family from the outside, you may judge them, thinking that none of them could be truly sane, since they cannot even agree about really important things for them. For them, however, it is good to remember and talk about it, because in this remembrance they connect with a sacred moment of their lives.

Perhaps "The Two Old Men" is a moralist story about always loving your brethren. I think, however, that the story is also about something else: Truth and Love. This Truth can never be fully encapsulated in statements, but it can always be perceived in the renewed lives of the beloved.

In his *Pray for Brother Alexander*, Constantin Noica wrote about what he calls the spirit of exactness:

> In fact, the spirit of exactness is active everywhere, not only in the exact sciences. History, for example, can no longer be done without exactness. Man cannot bear to not know exactly what and how it happened. A French historian from last century, Ernest Renan, wanted to see exactly where and how Jesus Christ lived. He went to the holy places and proceeded scientifically to the reconstitution of the Event. You know what happened to him? He found the traces of Jesus from Nazareth, but he no longer found the traces of Jesus Christ.[4]

Tolstoy's story says something about the spirit opposed to exactness. But you cannot be exact about this spirit. Tolstoy's account of it is masterfully accomplished in just a few lines, where he shows a family arguing about the exact story of an event that saved them from certain death. Their arguing, however, takes place in the light,

---

4. Noica, *Pray for Brother Alexander*, 65.

during moments when they themselves take care of strangers and when they bask in the life that they had received through Love.

The Legend of Manole and Ana: Building a Church in One's Bones

IN THE ROMANIAN LEGEND of Manole and Ana, everything that the builders did during the day collapsed over night. The ruler of the land had asked Manole and his team to build the most beautiful church on earth, but he could not do it. He is cast into despair because the punishment for not achieving it was death. Manole is not ready to die; is he ready to build a church?

A voice from above tells him that only a human sacrifice could break the curse. In doing this, the voice from above shows Manole a mirror: you are not ready to give up yourself. How can you build a church? Manole does not see it, and so he decides with his team to sacrifice the first person who comes with food in the morning.

He prays to God to stop Ana, his wife, but Ana comes, overcoming all the storms sent her way. Ana is ready to die; the church can contain her body, for her body is already a church. Manole puts bricks around her body, and the church no longer collapses overnight.

What does it take to build a church? Perhaps a denial of the ego and an embodiment of others. Manole cannot do it. He cannot build the church because he has not yet given himself up. How can he build a boat for salvation if he cannot yet open himself to others?

Build up churches, said Fr. George Calciu once, in communist Romania.[1] He was imprisoned for it. The only thing he asked was to make from our own bodies boats for the salvation of others. Of all others.

Ana becomes a church. She is already one before her husband covers her body with bricks. Ana's bones are the bricks of the church: she already lives for the lives of others.

---

1. See Calciu, *Interviews*, 161. This is the second homily from a series of seven homilies to the youth delivered during the Great Lent in 1978. As a consequence, George Calciu was imprisoned by the Communist regime for a second time.

Giving Thanks for Shortcomings

A FEW WEEKS AGO, during confession, I told my priest of a recurrent problem in my life, one that I do not seem to be able to escape. The priest said, "We all have one or several problems that are given to us, and if they are given to us, it is in them that we can find our salvation. If you cannot yet be free of this problem, perhaps it is in your fight with it that you can get closer to God." The priest did not say that I have to eliminate it for salvation but rather that I need to accept that I have it, to not see myself above it, and to see in it a blessing for which I need to give thanks: it is my chance to come closer to God. There is no despair, no matter how long we may fight with our shortcomings and no matter how many times we fall again.

Of course, the priest did not say that I don't have to do anything about it but rather that I should trust I would receive help to overcome it when the moment has come. Now, if I still have the problem with me, even if I fight it, perhaps I have not yet learned what I am to learn from it.

My priest's words still stay with me, and I often think of them. On the one hand, they gave me a certain joy: I am never alone on this path, but various energies are with me, some eating of my body, some nourishing it. And I have to give thanks to and for all of them. Then, there is something more to these words: if a shortcoming is a nail I put in Jesus' body, but it is also something that is given to me in the economy of salvation, how much love can there be in a gift that makes the giver suffer? What kind of love does God have if He allows me to do things that nail His body on the cross just because these things somehow may bring me to my salvation?

It Sounds Like Reason,
except that It Was a Choice

Socrates waits peacefully in prison for his death. Crito comes and offers him a choice: choose life, your friends, your sons. And it sounds like reason, except that it is a choice.

Antigone's brothers die on the battlefield: one defends the city; the other attacks it. So Creon, the new king, decides that one of them should be buried with honors, while the other would be left on the field, his corpse as prey for dogs and vultures. Antigone goes against the law and buries her brother. She chooses family and love, one may say. And it sounds like reason, except that it is a choice.

Imagine being in the following situation: someone asks you to choose between death and giving up God. You say, "I choose God." And it seems like the right choice, the choice of a martyr, except that it is a choice.

I summarized here possible situations in which we can talk about choice.

It seems there are two different realms here. In the first one, we talk meaningfully about choices. We often say that a choice is preferable, that we appreciate the moral value of an action, and so on. If our children make a debatable choice, it pains us, and we suffer together with them. If we are betrayed, we deplore not only the situation in which we find ourselves but also the poor state of the soul of the one who betrayed us. And, if we think about the examples above, many people side with Antigone and her love for her brother. They praise her courage to stand against the law and fight for the ones who can no longer fight for themselves.

Our hearts may take courage when we hear that someone chose God and was not afraid of death. For we know that he chose the good.

But can one *choose* the good? Perhaps the difference is truly between these two realms: in the one of choice, our actions may be more or less likeable, more or less valuable, with more or less positive consequences. Choice reveals one thing: that we believe we are the masters of our destiny. There is an important difference between choosing to become a torturer or not. But in the end, it still is a choice that may say that I became my own idol. When I choose, I choose the ego.

There is no choice for Socrates to run from prison. If he runs from prison, Socrates is no longer Socrates but a lover of the ego.

One more story. After being in the prison of Pitesti, the place where the communists wanted to destroy the souls of the Romanian youth, Fr. Calciu was sent to Jilava, a prison underground, in a cell with no windows. "We had an electric bulb, day and night. They put four of us in each cell. In each cell there would be either a very sick man or a mad man." It was a recipe for annihilation. The first day he enters the cell, one of the other three, Constantine (Costache) Oprisan, "whose lungs were completely emaciated by tuberculosis," begins to cough up the fluid in his lung. Fr. Calciu narrates: "I was leaning against the door, surprised because I had never seen anything like that. The man was suffocating. Perhaps a whole liter of phlegm and blood came up, and my stomach became upset. I was ready to vomit."[1] At this moment, two words made a miracle: "Constantine Oprisan noticed this and said to me, 'Forgive me.' I was so ashamed! Since I was a student in medicine, I decided then to take care of him."

It is the beginning of a process in which a soul that went through hell—and Pitesti was nothing short of hell—is cured. The beginning may have been a choice: he decides to take care of someone else. But this choice makes way for an inner rebirth, to

---

1. Calciu, *Interviews*, 109.

the point where one can say, "I don't choose God. But if I am to remain what I am, I cannot respond any other way than giving myself up. For this is what I am: a nobody for whom Someone is on the cross."

Presence is not a choice. Choice results in a lack of it.

A Lonely Superhuman with Simple Arithmetic

In Dostoevsky's *Crime and Punishment*, one of the characters wonders whether "thousands of good deeds will wipe out one little, insignificant transgression." The "insignificant" transgression is murder. "For one life taken, thousands saved from corruption and decay! One death, and a hundred lives in exchange—why, it's simple arithmetic!"[1] The same question troubles the main character, Raskolnikov.

The first reaction to such a question may be abhorrence. The lack of consideration for another human's life seems the attribute of brutes. Such attitudes, one may say, are absent in a civilized world, and only a deranged human being would disregard the life of another to such an extent. However, as we too often discover, this idea is prevalent precisely in modern "civilization" because modernity usually entertains the thought that it can beautify the world according to its own principles.

The "arithmetic" becomes terrifying when it is applied to political regimes. They have brought death to millions in the name of creating a new order. Nazism and communism claimed the superiority of a new man, the Aryan or the Worker, respectively. For their victory, the others were just expendable numbers.

It is easy to say that such regimes are evil. But aren't we, on our individual levels, expressing the same attitude toward the world when we apply this simple arithmetic? "The world would be

---

1. Dostoevsky, *Crime and Punishment*, 62.

just fine if 'that country' did not belong to it." "My country would be just fine if 'this kind of people' did not belong to it" (this is especially applicable to election seasons). "My family would be just fine if it weren't for that crazy uncle." In each of these situations I murder something: a country, a group of people, or a person. They become expendable for me. I would be happy if my world did not contain them. And it would be for the "good," for it would increase the beauty of *my* world. Beauty minus ugliness equals just beauty. It's simple "arithmetic." So it feels as if I have a responsibility for accomplishing this arithmetic.

By these "simple" thoughts, I have already committed murder. The first one who died is me, for I have extracted myself from the world given to me, and I have created one for me alone, according to my views. In doing so, I have destroyed my constellations: the bodies that I form with other persons in relationships. Martin Buber is often cited for two types of relationships: I-thou, in which the other human being is an infinite person with whom I enter an infinite relationship, and I-it, in which the other human being becomes an object and is used merely for the function that he or she may perform in the relationship. But we forget that in the I-it mode of existence there is no "I." The "I"—a person—can only be an "I" with other "I"s. When "I" relate to an it, "I" am no longer a person but an object myself. "I" have already created a world for myself, and I am alone in it: a murderer. The world that has been given to me has died; the persons who were in my world have died; I have died as person and have become an individual. I have died to life, but I continue to exist: a lonely superman with simple arithmetic.

Begin with ideology of any kind, and you are one step away from murder.

"There Was No Other Choice"

LET ME TELL YOU a story. After fighting as a soldier for his country, a young man returns home. There is nothing special about him; he did what was required of him, like many others who lived through or died in WWII. He was wounded and decorated—again, like many others. When he comes back home, he wants to establish a family, so he goes from village to village thinking that he may fall in love. And he does. One of his friends recounts, "He chose as wife a sixteen years old girl, small, who just entered the traditional winter meetings. She was happy, so happy that she forgot to cry when the wedding chariot took her to his place."

It is a love story: the two young people build together a life, they have a first child, and the young wife expects a second one. But this is when history strikes. The story takes place in Romania, after WWII. Romanians, just like the majority of Eastern Europeans, were beginning to experience another calamity: the communist persecution.

But this story is not about persecution; it is about this man who, with an expecting young wife and a toddler, runs away from home and hides in the mountains when the Securitate, the communist secret police in Romania, is looking for him. He was one of the wealthier people of his village, which back then meant that you had some land or some craft that allowed you to have your own workshop, and he had been labeled an "enemy of the people." The point is that he runs from home, leaving his wife behind while knowing what it meant for her and her young child: beatings, arrests, and loss of any chance to have a secure life (the Securitate could throw you into a dungeon without any warrant and without any trial; in the late 1940s and early 1950s, many were even shot with a bullet in the back of the head because they did not give up their land).

A young man runs away to hide for his life, leaving behind his pregnant wife and his child.

"A coward," some of my students said when they heard this story. How can you leave your wife behind? Stay home, go to prison, even die if this is required of you, but do not give up your responsibility for your family.

One could defend this man in many ways. For example, one may say that there was no other solution. Even if he stayed at home, his family was still the family of a "bandit," as these people were labeled by the communists. It was still a family of "an enemy of the people," and this meant that his wife would still not be accepted for work, his children would still not be accepted in universities. At least he could fight if he went into the mountains, do something to get rid of the persecutors—and he was, indeed, part of the anti-communist resistance movement.

But this is not an explanation, I think. Indeed, he had no choice but not because other choices were not better. There was no other choice because there is no choice. Choice had nothing to do with the results of his actions. He had no choice because the man who loved the young woman who was "so happy, so happy that she forgot to cry" when she got married, that man would have died in the absence of freedom. He would no longer have been a person but an individual, an object like any other, a "brick," as Fr. Calciu says, in the mighty construction that communism wanted to realize in Romania.[1] A brick can be replaced with other bricks. Its relations with others have no personal characteristics. Gheorghe Haşu the person did not leave his wife because he chose a value that was higher than his love for her. It is in this love for her that he acted the way he did. For love has no purpose. Love has no end. Love is not for something that comes after it, a life with children

---

1. Calciu, *Interviews*, 162.

and grandchildren. Love is its own child. And to this love both of them were faithful. This does not mean that they were faithful to something else other than them, but rather to "Eugenia and Gheorghe together."

I wondered how I could explain to my students what happened with the people who fought against communism in the anti-communist resistance. One day, as I often do, I was listening to country music. And I fell upon a song, Carrie Underwood's "Just a Dream." Prior to a particular performance of this song, a young woman speaks of her deceased husband. He was a soldier, and he died in the war. He died for his own country. His wife could receive the honor that he deserved; she could cry about his loss openly; she would be respected by her peers; she would not have to hide everything that would remind of him; her children would not be persecuted and called their entire lives the "children of a bandit." And nobody would say that her husband left her behind when she was young and she had a toddler.

Gheorghe Hașu did the same thing. He fought for his country, which means his family, his wife, and his children. But his country had already been stolen, so nobody acknowledged his fight.

Before his arrest that led to his eventual execution, Gheorghe sent his wife a short verbal message through a courier: "Tell her to forgive me. And to raise the children as God will help her."

This request for forgiveness does not need a response. It is only the expression of being with the other.

"There Was No Other Choice"

Gheorghe Haşu was caught by the Securitate after being betrayed; he was then tried and executed.

In a recent interview, Eugenia Haşu said, "he was a good husband, he loved me; I had no problems with him." She and her two children survived the persecution. She died of old age, surrounded in love.

"Christ Is Risen!" Now . . . What?

TODAY IS THE SUNDAY of the Resurrection for Orthodox Christians. It comes at the end of the Holy Week, the most beautiful period of the entire year. Its beauty stems precisely from the Sunday that comes at its end, because you live every moment waiting for the Resurrection. It is a very emotional week; with every Bridegroom service, every presanctified liturgy, the Holy Unction of Wednesday, the washing of the feet, the Last Supper, the lowering from the cross and the Lamentations of Friday, you walk with Christ on an excruciating path. Even if you spend hours upon hours in church, I don't know of a more productive week, and I truly believe this is so because, although you may believe you walk with Christ, it is He who walks with you. Participating in the act in which God glorifies himself, on the cross (!!!) out of love for us, you are given the opportunity to be in your highest moment of your humanity: being with another in his or her suffering. It is mysterious how you're not tired, even if you sleep less, how you're joyful, even if you're crying, and how you wish Holy Week would never end, even if you thirst for the Resurrection.

During the week, you are reminded of Jesus' words in the garden of Gethsemane: "So, could you not watch with me one hour?" You then try to be more present and more watchful. It is indeed a week of presence and watchfulness, and all of your senses seem to be awake.

But Sunday comes and with it immense joy. The gates of Hades are broken, and death cannot contain the One who has no beginning. "Christ is risen from the dead, trampling down death by death, and upon those in the tombs bestowing life."

Christ is Risen!

So is it that I can now go to sleep? . . .

It certainly feels so, and it feels so as a loss. I no longer need to be watchful, but I can rejoice. I no longer need to pay heed to live every moment of my life because now I am in the Resurrection. This attitude reflects a Platonism (and I think Plato was not a Platonist, but this is a different discussion) that divides life into two: we expect to die so we finally live. Fr. Stephen Freeman often writes about it. In other words, we do something for the sake of something else. Here is an example: we fast, so we are forgiven, which is perhaps one of the most pernicious understanding of fasting.

Even for Plato, philosophy is the practice for death and dying, that is for the daily renunciation of one's self. It is in this dying to myself that I truly live.

Perhaps even this question, "Now what?," is the manifestation of my not-complete dying. If I truly emptied myself, then I may live the Resurrection while still being on the cross. I continue to be sick, but I am also full, because Christ is risen! I am weak, but I am also strong, because Christ is risen! I am lost, but I am also found, because Christ is risen!

So let us rejoice in the Resurrection! But let us not forget that tomorrow St. George is celebrated, so we have liturgy. Then a Sunday follows every other seven days. And this means work: liturghia!

Let me also remember I have dishes to wash; I have papers to grade; I know people in suffering. Let me continue to embrace the Joy that embraces me! So let me rejoice in work!

Christ is risen!

Ode to My Wife

I HAD A MOMENT of weakness this morning. I was running here and there, being mentally preoccupied with the many things to do, and I went to the bathroom to brush my teeth before leaving home. My wife was already there. I took a deep breath, I felt everything coming over me, and I said, "The truth is, I am finished."

The moment of weakness passed by the time I was done brushing my teeth, and I began dealing step-by-step with the various things that were overwhelming me. But it just dawned on me that the one person who suffers with me through all of my ups and downs, regardless of whether she is fully aware of them or not, is my wife. Both of us often spare the other of the various challenges that we have on the path. Nevertheless, before her, I am always naked: she sees when I come angry from work, when I fall down and say, "I am finished," or when my hair slowly disappears from my scalp. She lives through my changes of career, my loss of physical strength (after forty, you consider it a blessing being able to spend a couple of hours on a soccer pitch and not getting injured by the end), or my various whims over the day. It's not that she takes on my duties; there is no need for such thing. It's rather that she stays with me through it all. She bears my cross by staying in my life.

This is not about the virtues my wife has. Nor about the things she does for me. It is rather about one weak human being who took upon herself a life that is touched every moment by the weaknesses of someone who was once a stranger to her: me.

Ode to My Wife

My wife is, in many ways, my priest. And let me say it again: before her, I am always naked, just as I am, without any fears: the similar natures of love and heaven.

The Canon of Joy

SOME YEARS AGO, WHEN an older lady went to church for the last time prior to no longer being able to leave her place, she asked the priest what else she could do. And the priest said, "I give you the canon to have joy!"

Now just think about this: a canon of joy! Your feet no longer help you to move out of your house: JOY! You see how, one by one, your friends disappear: JOY! Your body tells you that your remaining moments on earth will be painful: JOY!

How can you make yourself have joy? Especially in the context of a canon, this seems to be quite difficult. It requires an effort: you have to make yourself stop for a minute and remember to be joyful. But how do you stop in order to practice rejoicing? And what does this mean?

A while ago, I was stopped on the campus's streets by some young college students. There were two girls and a boy, dressed very casually, like anyone else on campus, but who asked with the air of importance that only a life or death question can give you: "What do you think will happen to your soul when you die?" They belonged to some Christian organization, and they clearly had in mind that they were responsible for the salvation of my soul—that is, they had the power to save me.

The Canon of Joy

Back then, I was writing my dissertation on Aristotle's notion of soul, so I could not resist the temptation to begin a dialogue with them. "Tell me what you mean by 'soul' and I may tell you what I think will happen to it when I die." To my regret, the conversation was very short. I think they may have written me off as one of the lost souls of the philosophers that are mentioned in the Bible, so my young interlocutors excused themselves and looked around for another victim.

I remembered this scene due to a comment from a fellow Orthodox. He said, "There are many sayings of the fathers I see tossed around by Orthodox in the ways that Protestants toss Bible verses around. Many of these 'Orthodox memes of encouragement' seem like vipers to me. They say things like, 'Once one has experienced Christ then they know nothing but joy!' – Some Elder of Some Famous Monastery. But I can only read such things in reverse . . . since I know much that is not joy, I must not have experienced Christ."

The experience he described, that "these memes of encouragement seem like vipers" to him, was very similar to my own feelings of despair whenever people stopped me on my path to ask me whether my soul was saved. Such "events" come always as a nuisance. And even more, what does it mean to tell people that they must rejoice? Or that they must consider the status of their souls?

Truly nothing! My fellow was, after all, right. Words do not do anything. Words about joy are just moral encouragements to be in a way in which you may not be able to function at a certain moment. They miss the point. You can compare them to this situation: you burned your hand in the fire, come to me for help, and I respond, "Once you have experienced Christ, you know nothing but joy!" If this answer is the expression of joy, then joy can only be an oppression, and you would rightly not want to do anything with it.

However, I've been in the presence of people whose joy was oppressing, but it was not oppressing to me, but rather to my shortcomings. These people did not speak about this joy, because there was no need for them to say words to make it present. In its presence, any kind of oppression was disappearing. This is because their joy could fill the emptiness of my spiritual weakness. They were not out to save me, but they were living life as if already in the Kingdom, so in joy.

But don't get me wrong: they were not like people on drugs. They were not dancing in the rain, nor were they singing praises to the Lord—at least not outwardly. They were rather caring for someone whose hand was burned, were making coffee for someone who was tired, or were cutting firewood for winter.

The miracle was that I was also in the Kingdom because of their joy. Me, the one without joy, already embraced by the Joy that lived in them.

Hoarders of Ideas

If I remember correctly, Fr. Thomas Hopko once said that we can consider our minds similar to a room. The pieces of furniture in these rooms are ideas—not the Platonic ones but ideas that we form by our interaction with the environment. During a human life, even if we speak of wealthy young men, as the Stranger calls them in *The Sophist*, these ideas shape the room. Because of their various sources, they often do not match each other, just as when we buy furniture at different moments in time and from different stores without considering what we have previously bought and what we have inherited or received as a gift. The purpose of a sophist, at least according to Plato, seems to be to create more stuff that humans can buy, so that their souls are filled to the point of overflowing. The effect is disastrous for a human being: it is ignorance of the worst kind, when people have no knowledge but believe they know. They fall in love with the furniture of their rooms, and the feeling of safety that this love provides precludes them from going out in the world, to find truth. Each one becomes his or her own god. Filling their rooms with more and more furniture, they can no longer see outside it and are no longer able to come out of the door, for there is no door: it has been covered with pieces of furniture. There are no windows, for they have been covered as well by the multitude of the pieces of furniture that populate the room.

It is the image of a hoarder but one who is not aware of one's own hoarder-ness. It is also the manifestation of a disease and of ugliness, and so we may say that one needs purification. But a sophist, at least according to Plato's dialogue *The Sophist*, does not consider curing the people he interacts with. It would be to his disadvantage to do so. He is not a hoarder, but he is producing that which the hoarder buys. The main difference between him and a consumer is that a sophist realizes what the soul is: a place for ideas. In order to get ahead in this world, he creates them. He brings them to life, and he makes others live in them. If he is a good merchant, he needs to understand how his customers work, and their hoarder-ness makes his business thrive. Confusion and lack of clarity provide his element; as consequence, he is hard to be grasped, because he has learned to be anything. As we see in Plato's *The Sophist*, even if the impression is that consumers deal with him, they deal only with his appearance, and so they get entangled within a world that is not.

But then there is the one who engages in refutation. In *The Sophist*, this guy seems to be a sophist as well, for he engages in the art of refutation, the elenchus, the "greatest and most authoritative of purifications" (230d). It is the Socratic art of questioning, in which he examines opinions with ease, brings them together in the same place, puts them side by side one another, "and in so putting them he shows that the opinions are simultaneously contrary to themselves about the same things in regard to the same things in the same respects" (230b). Or that we are hoarders. The art of purification has beauty as result. As the Stranger puts it, "One must hold in turn that whoever's unrefuted, even if he is in fact the great king, if he is unpurified in the greatest things, has become uneducated and ugly in those things in which it was fitting for whoever will be in his being happy to be purest and most beautiful" (230d-e).

Is the refuter a sophist? He appears as one who engages in debates for the sake of debating. How often do we hear that Socrates is just a guy who likes to hear himself talking and who engages in fruitless discussion? It shows how easy it is to perceive the work of refutation as the work of sophistry. After all, the Stranger claims in the dialogue that the philosopher and the sophist are both difficult to see vividly, so there is a connection but in two different ways. "The philosopher," he says, "devoted to the idea of that which is always through calculations, it's on account of the brilliance of the place that he's in no way easy to be seen, for the eyes of the soul of the many are incapable of keeping up a steady gaze on the divine" (254a). The sophist is "a fugitive into the darkling of 'that which is not,' to which he attaches himself by a knack, and on account of the darkness of the region, he's hard to get an understanding of" (254a). So perhaps the purpose of each could not be more opposed. Refutation cleanses the soul of ideas. It shows that all these pieces of furniture do not match, that our rooms are ugly, regardless of the beauty of any piece of furniture that we may have there by mistake. On the contrary, sophistry creates more and more stuff and encourages a consumer society.

So perhaps there are two activities for a philosopher: refutation and dialectics. What connects them is that a philosopher is in both of them the agent of bringing to light that which is already present. In the case of refutation, it is the disease that is revealed so it can be eliminated. A philosopher would not replace the previous stuff with anything else. In Socrates's words from the *Meno*, he numbs others because he is numb himself. But even if his numbness is not to be understood as complete emptiness, a philosopher knows that what he has is not his. Rather, he has the privilege of discovering it. And, through refutation, he places others in the possibility to discover it themselves, or to engage in dialectic. For in dialectic, a philosopher no longer interacts with others but remains by himself, in a work of contemplation in the region of the divine, where one brings nothing with oneself because everything is already present, although in a hidden manner. Dialectic reveals the beauty of eternal ideas.

A philosopher and a sophist both work with the souls of others, at least when dialectic is not involved. In their interactions with them, something happens: something comes to be. The lack of interest in truth and the presence of some awareness about how to catch others make the sophist produce that which is not, so it can be sold. The love for truth in a philosopher sends him into a work of revealing: first, revealing disease in those who have consumed not-being, second revealing beauty, even if it cannot be seen if one has not submitted oneself to refutation. It is, after all, a manifestation of material culture, for a philosopher seems to become the incarnation of the region of the forms: if they are to be visible, they are visible in him. He has a grasp of the divine, and he possibly manifests it. A sophist, having no grasp of the divine, presents himself as such, but does so to the level of perception of others. If we study them, we realize that philosophers and sophists are hard to grasp. A philosopher reveals things, and, by consequence, he is not seen because of the brilliance of the region that is revealed. The sophist produces things, and, by consequence, he is not seen because of the darkness of the region that he produces.

It's the first Sunday of Lent, and I spend it in traveling from a conference on Greek philosophy. A bit ironic, I would say. It is the Sunday of Orthodoxy, in which people bring icons, to celebrate the faith. Icons that somehow make the Kingdom present. And I talked about the sophist, who instead of making the Kingdom present, that is, allowing it to come to life in him, creates images and presents them as the real Kingdom. *The Sophist* as a clarification between iconodules and iconoclasts . . . The iconoclasts reject the iconodules because, ironically, they do not accept the possibility of speech. It is ironic, for doing so they speak from the realm of non-being.

Isn't life in dialectic tuning yourself in to the music of ideas? Or perhaps singing like a bird and so allowing the Song to come to be in your particular voice?

Incomplete Morning Thought on Heaven

I USED TO ASK myself this question: "What will you do if you go to heaven and find Stalin there? Will you tell God, 'Sorry, but this is not the place for me'?"

The question was mistaken.

The challenge is not to accept "my enemies" in heaven if God brings them there but to accept that I can be in heaven only if I have already accepted them. There is no heaven for me in their absence; they participate in the world and are part of my constellations. If heaven does not include Stalin, this is not because I do not accept him there; if I don't accept him, I am not in heaven myself. Stalin's absence, if such is the case, results from the fact that he cannot accept himself: the all-encompassing love burns the one who cannot accept this love.

This is why heaven is also a place of mourning, for you cannot be in heaven without mourning the absence of those who are loved regardless of their worthlessness and who cannot accept freely this love.

Accepting Stalin in heaven does not mean accepting the evil manifested in him. Accepting him presupposes fighting him as he is.

Time and Eternity

PHILOSOPHERS PERCEIVE ETERNITY AS something unmoved—the unmoved mover of Aristotle. But Dumitru Stăniloae says that eternity cannot be just an unmoved substance—this is death. Life is activity and movement. And so eternity itself, which is life, is also activity and movement. The one activity and movement that we can understand as being part of divinity is love. Stăniloae says, "The true meaning of eternity can be found only in the perfect communion which subsists between eternal Persons whose love is inexhaustible."[1] Persons are not immovable; in their interconnections, there is a constant and inexhaustible renewal of love.

So, if we do not understand eternity in a strictly philosophical fashion, as something unchangeable but rather as something that goes beyond our notions of rest and change—and this is love itself—then we can see, Stăniloae says, that time and eternity are compatible.

Time is not a sin against eternity. It is not as if we were in eternity, fell from it at the beginning of creation, and are waiting for our time to be received back in eternity. Time has not begun with the Fall, and thus it is not opposed to eternity. In fact, Fr. Stăniloae says, the Eternity of God, Love between the Persons of the Trinity who are perfectly in union, carries time within itself.

How does eternity carry time within itself? Stăniloae says that God enters into a relationship with temporal beings, with us, in our own reality of time, waiting for each of us to give a response.

1. Stăniloae, *Eternity and Time*, 2.

Time and Eternity

Communication is personal, so we all have our own times. If God enters a relationship with temporal beings, this is because all things begin with him and also end with him, and time is the interval for the response that we each need to enter, by grace, in communion with God.

Here's a beautiful quote from Fr. Stăniloae: "Love is the gift of oneself to another, and the waiting for the full return of that gift from the other in response [...] The interval of waiting for the response is time. As such, time represents a spiritual distance between persons, while eternity is beyond all distance or separation."[2]

But I want to emphasize that time is a spiritual distance which has orientation. God offers to us his love, orienting us toward him, in proportion of our growth, so through our slow response, we can rejoin him, by grace, in eternity.

The idea of orientation is important, and I will talk about it by mentioning prison and persecution. Fr. Stăniloae was in communist prisons. When someone persecutes you, he gives you a different orientation; he arrests you in the sense that he redefines your world in connection with him only. In terror, you are fully focused on the danger coming from your persecutor, and you exist only in his world. Under torture, it is difficult to think of God and of your love for your neighbor. Fr. Roman Braga, who was in a terrible prison in Pitești, where friends were forced to torture their own friends, said that he encountered the devil in Pitești but God in solitary confinement. What comes to life in you in the presence of your enemy is nothingness—no connection. The enemy takes you away from any connection you have with others, so with love, because he places you on a terrifying pedestal. The enemy tells you that you belong to his world. YOU are the one who must be tortured. In this way, he gives you an orientation and a different kind of eternity, the eternity of separation and loss, in which there is no connection with anyone else.

So there are two types of eternity: one of love, and one of pain and suffering. In fact, Fr. Stăniloae says that "time is like the distance between the two ends of a bridge. There is something

---

2. Stăniloae, *Eternity and Time*, 3.

ambiguous, uncertain about it. It is a state of movement in the direction either of death or fullness of life." Death and fullness of life are not the two ends of the bridge. Both ends are in God, at the end of the journey on the bridge. You begin with God at the beginning of the bridge, you are given an orientation, but on this long journey of the bridge of life you are brought to the reality that the enemy forces you toward a different orientation. The enemy makes you focus on yourself because he makes you defend yourself. The enemy cancels your personhood. He restructures your cosmos, he defines you, and he tells you that you can only exist on one level only, that of a victim. He makes you focus on yourself, and he cancels all personhood, and you remain alone. The danger is that, on this bridge of life, we end up in the constant refusal of love. Here's Stăniloae again: "A constant refusal to respond to the offer of love fixes the creature spiritually in the total impossibility of communication. Here there is no more waiting, no more hope, no more expectation."[3] It is a different type of eternity, one that has no time and no genuine eternity.

So death and fullness of life, both of them, are in God. Eternity is either that of death, because you are no longer able to love anymore, or the eternity of life, in your full response to Love.

It seems that time and eternity remind us that the highest challenge we have in life is the ability to respond to love, especially when things around us (because of torture or pleasure) encourage us to focus on ourselves. Life is an attempt to walk on the bridge of time, living in the hope that at the end we will experience what we have lived, in part, on the bridge as well: the eternity of God's love. On the bridge, this is experienced in the gift that our lives become for the lives of others.

The love of a genuine person is a gift that offers orientation. The connection that Alyosha provides in his presence opens him up to others, but it also opens the possibility of life in the kingdom for them. Their response to Alyosha is the creation of a new life within their souls.

---

3. Stăniloae, *Eternity and Time*, 10.

The Gift of Failure

IN ONE OF AESOP's fables, two travelers find a place of rest on a hot day under a plane tree.[1] One of them remarks on the uselessness of the tree: its existence is governed by failure, since it has no fruit. The tree is vexed about the ingratitude of the traveler, who cannot see the benefit he receives from its shade. The plane tree appears again in Plato, in a dialogue where Socrates invites Phaedrus to deliver his speech about love under a plane tree. The *Phaedrus* is a dialogue where two arts and their respective pedagogies are placed face-to-face. On the one hand, sophistry, which claims to give its students measurable knowledge. On the other hand, Socratic philosophy, which is often accused of having nothing to offer to the measurable, objective world. Why the plain tree, though? It may be that ancient writers were fascinated with the ingratitude of human beings, who, while benefiting from the world, reproach it for not giving them what it was never meant to give them. The plane tree is also the image of philosophy,[2] often accused of being sterile, because it does not produce anything palpable. Just consider Socrates's education, which begins with a most confusing claim: "I only know that I don't know anything." How many parents would send their children to a school that has such a claim on its frontispiece? While a hero for Plato, Socrates remains someone who produces no measurable outcome. Whether it is Euthyphro,

---

1. See the fable also referenced above, on page 3.
2. I heard this suggestion for the first time from Mark Gifford, whose ancient philosophy courses were a joy at Virginia Tech.

Ion, or Crito, Socrates's interlocutors do not leave wiser or open to learning after encountering him. By all human accounts, Socrates is a failure.

Socrates's singularity would suggest that failure is not a property applicable to human beings in general, at least clearly not an essential one. Failures are trees that offer no fruit. Failures are philosophers who, as someone once said, produce dust around a topic and are then surprised that things are no longer visible. We often think that some people are failures because of the activities in which they engage but not the species itself. After all, when Aristotle searched for the essence of human beings, failure never entered his mind as a candidate. In the process of distinguishing among species, he naturally searched for positive aspects, whether these features have to do with rationality or social behavior. And then there is Costică Brădăţan,[3] whose stories in his *In Praise of Failure: Four Lessons in Humility* lead to one unstated conclusion: a human is a creature whose life is defined by failure. So perhaps there is a Socrates in us, waiting to be born the moment when we realize what he knew 2500 years ago: attempt to know yourself, and you'll end up knowing nothing.

To be sure, there is no other animal that contemplates its own failure; when we say that animals "fail," we express our reading of the situation. We humans judge their actions against some perfect ideal. The lion "fails" to prey on an antelope in our eyes. For the lion itself, the unaccomplished action does not have the flavor of failure. This is because animals do not evaluate their actions in reference to a standard, nor do they contemplate what could be their ultimate failure, death; they just act. Humans have plans, desires, and also questions about the meaning of life or a perfectly happy life. Our being-toward something that is not yet manifested makes us beings governed by failure. After all, Brădăţan's book is always about a person's failure, regardless of the circle he describes: the person fails externally, politically, socially, and intimately. All things fail because we fail, because we understand the world in terms of failure.

3. Brădăţan, *In Praise of Failure*.

The Gift of Failure

Failure is a funny thing: it comes with that which is specifically ours, our personhood. Only persons, Cristos Yannaras says in *Person and Eros*, understand Being "as temporality, as a rising up to presence, and this means that the human person is the only being which 'stands out' (ex-istatai), which can 'stand outside' its being, that is, which can understand its being, as presence, as temporal 'nowness.'"[4] Be a person, and failure is with you regardless of whether you realize it or not. It governs all the moments of your life, even those of glory. Your successes take place under its shadow, and your evaluation of your and your world's existence rests upon it. Of course, "how we relate to failure defines us, while success is auxiliary and fleeting and does not reveal much,"[5] as Brădățan says. But failure is more than this: it is an essential ingredient to our minute evaluation of this existence. Of course, if you are a human being, you will fail. Even more, the way we respond to it will write the story of our life, but we have no escape from having to respond to it. But failure is much more than this: even a life filled with successes only (as if such a thing existed) will be governed by the possibility of having failed and by the certainty of our ultimate failure: death. As Fr. George Calciu once said, "You are the most unfortunate being on earth, for neither plants nor animals have any consciousness of life and death, but you do. You know that you live, and you especially know that you will die. Your whole life unfolds under the somber perspective of death."[6]

Some may say that the Heraclitean existence of our world makes us participate in failure: everything changes; what has a beginning has an end. However, Heraclitus cannot produce thoughts about incompleteness without referencing completeness. We need Parmenides's perfection to see Heraclitus's world as the one of failure. The world does not embody failure; we do. This is because while we live in a changing world, we thirst for Parmenides's unchanging one.

4. Yannaras, *Person and Eros*, 32.
5. Brădățan, *In Praise of Failure*, 3.
6. Calciu, *Interviews*, 182. This is part of the sixth homily to the youth previously referenced.

The Greeks saw the entire life as part of becoming. They didn't call becoming "participation in failure"; however, becoming is nothing else than changing at all times without ever reaching a status of final completion. This is not problematic as long as nobody is searching for that state of completion. But since we all desire *eudaimonia*, which is expressed in an excellent, complete life, we are bound to fail. If we bring Brădățan and Aristotle together, this is what humans are: those beings who search their entire lives for excellence while being doomed to never have it.

Brădățan's heritage is not Greek but Romanian. If this were any other kind of book, his Romanian heritage may be just an unimportant biographical detail. But Romanians are, as he mentions, particularly good at failure. It's not that failure is ever-present in Romania, or that we, Romanians, believe we are good at failing, as Brădățan himself reminds us. It is more that we delight in it. There is nothing like the pleasure of telling yourself that you will never be able to do it, that everything you have done to reach a certain stage can only show that you qualified for nothing, since inevitably you will fail. And you fail because you don't truly want anything, caught in the eternity given by what some call the Romanian ethos. "Eternity was born in Romanian villages," Lucian Blaga, a Romanian philosopher and poet of the 20th century, used to say. E. M. Cioran, a contemporary of Blaga and one of the historical figures discussed in Brădățan's book, was cast into despair by the ability of his nation to excel in lacking excellence.

Failure is always embodied; it never comes up abstractly on Brădățan's pages, flying around conceptually, being thirsty for a definition. Instead, from Simone Weil's failures, to Ghandi's, to Cioran's, to a people's, or to Kimitake Hiraoka's, failure flares up in its multitude. For "failure is boundless, and its manifestations legion."[7] Failure is the shadow from which we all run but also that which gives substance to our lives: what kind of beings would we be if we were not governed by failure? Even "from God's point of view, the existence of the world is an embarrassment."[8] Perhaps this

7. Brădățan, *In Praise of Failure*, 7.
8. Brădățan, *In Praise of Failure*, 11.

is what the point of failure is: if it is part of who we are, running from it is a fight against one's nature.

The fact that we cannot escape it stems from our eternal search for meaning. And since modernity has left God in the shadows, Brădățan says that "people will flock to the charismatic politician who gives them even an illusion of meaning. They will swallow up anything from him, even the silliest bilge, and imagine him a savior."[9] Isn't it spectacular that anytime we run away from failure, we end up in an even bigger one?

Sure, the question comes: if we cannot run from failure, why don't we embrace it? Why don't we embrace our ultimate reality, the scariest of them all: we are limited beings? Much more difficult to do it than to think about it.

Be that as it may, life may turn out to be quite boring if failure were not part of it. Failure allows us to be new: to see life with new eyes. For the one who experiences failure, the world is born again. "Old presumptions are shattered," Brădățan writes, "certainties fade away, reputable truths are put to shame."[10] This does not mean that you should encourage others to fail. You cannot ask them to do what they cannot escape from doing. And you should not even encourage them to accept their fate. Accepting the humility coming from failure can only be a lesson that you make yourself listen to. Otherwise, when was anyone capable of doing this because of failure? Ask Socrates, who offered plenty of opportunities to his interlocutors to humble themselves. The only fruit of his seeds was the hemlock that he had to drink himself.

When he said that philosophy is preparation for death and dying, Socrates may have meant that philosophy makes you humble because it gives you awareness that human knowledge is incomplete. Just like failure, philosophy may cure from what Brădățan calls "the umbilicus mundi syndrome, a pathological inclination to place ourselves at the center of everything, and to fancy ourselves far more important than we are."[11] Even so, philos-

---

9. Brădățan, *In Praise of Failure*, 61.
10. Brădățan, *In Praise of Failure*, 31.
11. Brădățan, *In Praise of Failure*, 42.

ophy, just like failure, remains a medication that one can prescribe to oneself only. This is what makes Simone Weil great: she administers her own medication, or she preaches what she is willing to do herself. She doesn't tell others that they should join the ranks of the poor; instead, she witnesses what people go through, and she takes their burden upon her shoulders. She works in a factory, assuming what she sees as the condition of a slave; she takes "death as a matter of philosophical conviction and personal conviction."[12] For a person who is already physically weak, as Weil, working in a factory can only increase daily difficulties. Everything about her can be deemed personal failures. These failures lead you to humility and, like Weil, to Christ, but they cannot be prescribed. If you give them to others as solutions, either on an intimate level, like Socrates does, or on a social level, like dictators who believe they are the world's saviors, you create monsters and victims.

This is especially the case in the political realm. The Nazis and the communists, the two regimes that produced the humanitarian disasters of the 20th century in Europe, began with the desire to transform a failed humanity into a new, better one. The idea of the new man imposed from above can only be murderous. Perhaps there is no better example than the French Revolution that ended in the Reign of Terror, "born ironically out of a great love of humanity,"[13] as Brădățan rightly points out. The Bolsheviks wanted to create a society in which they would eliminate the failures coming from inequality. The Nazis wanted a superior human being. They all left behind them millions of dead bodies. Human beings cannot be transformed into a different kind of being; the only aspect in which they may be perfect is failure.

Still, there are always people who fall in love with political approaches that want to cure humanity of its essential imperfection. The attraction that dictators of all flavors bring before the simple masses is the promise that they would escape them from themselves. A Lenin resolves all problems, because he helps you bring to light a new man. A Hitler redeems you because he renders

12. Brădățan, *In Praise of Failure*, 45.
13. Brădățan, *In Praise of Failure*, 89.

dignity back to your people. Fascinated by their powers and their promises of a heavenly but still earthy humanity, you dance with them in the drunkenness produced by the bottles of promised perfection. When you wake up, you realize that the earth under your feet is still moving, covered by bodies who take their last breath, and you cannot realize why your bloody hand holds a gun.

The political failure belongs to those who fought against failure: the Nazis and the communists, the so-called enemies of the darkest age of the 20th century, fight against what they define as failure. Their approach is identical; the details differ. Any totalitarian regime defines the mightiness of the nation, creating boundaries for it and eliminating the elements that do not belong to it, internal or external. Regardless of what perfect ideas we create as idols, we will always leave behind us a pile of dead bodies. Brădățan's warning is accurate: "Be careful what you wish for!" Think of anything: classless society, ideal state, equality—"They are all admirable, as lofty as they are well-meaning, but we should never lose sight of what they are: political fictions. Not some mended version of the real world, but a wild act of imagination—a world unto itself, almost completely cut off from political reality."[14]

The mirage that political extremes had over intellectuals, be them on the left (think France) or on the right (think Romania), has to do with the hope of recreating a humanity free of failure. Among them, Emil Cioran's case is particularly attractive. Despaired of Romania's perennial failure, he has no problem to be a failure himself. On the contrary: he delights in it as if it were the only virtue to obtain on this earth. Strange thing being despaired of the failure of the nation to which you belong but delighted in your own failure. Brădățan doesn't miss the paradox: he writes about Cioran in a section on social failure.

Cioran lived and wrote in Romania between the two wars of 20th century. If Blaga was fascinated by the eternity experienced in a Romanian village, Cioran was cast into despair by it. The strength manifested by extremist movements came in direct contrast with a space where nothing used to take place. Cioran was ready to

---

14. Brădățan, *In Praise of Failure*, 120.

give up eternity for a glorious moment, regardless of its violence. Villages have no place in history. They are repetitive, like eternity. Think of an old man in a village of Transylvania, Cioran's birthplace, looking at the birds in the sky and judging that rain comes tomorrow. He would wake up in the morning, feed the chickens, and go light a candle at the tomb of his parents. He may then work his garden and quarrel with his neighbor. In the evening, he would kneel before a candle, pray for his children and for his good departure from this world, and thank God for the blessings of the day. The following day he would start again, following the seasons of the year but also the cyclical seasons of the church in his village: great Lent, Pascha, Ascension, Pentecost . . . and again the following year. How do you become a perfectionist in failure after you are surrounded by such an atmosphere? Perhaps you must be the son of a priest, like Cioran, and play with skulls in cemeteries as a child.

A book about failure must end with death: our ultimate failure. But why would it be our failure since we share it with all living things? Perhaps death is not a failure; our approach to it makes it so. Cioran is not the hero of this chapter. He "berated the universe all his life, and sang lavish praises to self-annihilation, but he forgot to kill himself when the time came."[15] Yukio Mishima and Jean Amery did not. They even attempted it several times, failing at the act of ultimate failure; when they succeeded, failure was no more.

One may wonder: why would a book on failure end with suicide, this attempt to end all humiliating failures and us as humans at the same time? Why not return to Dostoevsky's Grand Inquisitor, who accuses Christ of the failure to provide meaning to an entire humanity? Or to the death on the cross and his disciples' failure to initially recognize in it the ultimate redemption of failure in the renunciation of the will? You fail because you want to avoid it. Failure does teach humility. But genuine humility is not the opposite of success; it is the embracing of one's nature and being delighted in it.

---

15. Brădățan, *In Praise of Failure*, 198.

It may be because animals do not dispose of their own being. Our capacity to commit suicide is exclusively human. Cioran reminds us of it, and Brădăţan does not fail to point it out. The ability to fail and the ability to kill oneself: what kind of species are we that we distinguish ourselves from others by the capacity to evaluate our capacities and to end any capacity? One that remains what it is only if it embraces failure. *In Praise of Failure* praises our humanity the way it is. It shows that if we run from failure, we run from what makes us humans, and we become beasts. If we embrace it, we transcend it.

The Situation of the Earth

"I IMAGINE A SCHOOL where nothing is taught."[1] The words belong to, at the time, a young Romanian philosopher, Constantin Noica. The statement must have sounded odd, especially in 1935, during a period of time marked by certainties, be that to the right or to the left of the political spectrum. The statement remains odd regardless of when it is uttered. Knowledge and certainty are attractive, people say. Be confident, and people will want to work with you. It is not the shy and the uncertain who have followers but those who are capable of claiming their truth as the truth. Humility has never been a largely accepted virtue. If we are to believe the cynical, those who accept it do so because they are weak and they need it to make something out of their lives. In its absence, they would be too overwhelmed by the powerful, those who do not care so much about the truth but about showing their status in society because of the knowledge they have.

The idea of a school where nothing is learned shows how humility and knowledge are connected. Whether it begins with Socrates's famous claim that he only knows that he does not know anything, or even with the notion of a philosopher (someone who loves wisdom—*philia* + *sophia*—not someone who possesses it), there is an acknowledgement that genuine wisdom can only take place when someone also understands that his knowledge is not worth much in the great scheme of things.

---

1. Noica, *Jurnal filozofic*, 7.

The Situation of the Earth

Bellitto's *Humility: The Secret History of a Lost Virtue* reconfirms that the history of humility is inevitably connected to knowledge. This also means that it is connected with our attitude toward God, as the ultimate reality to be known. Whether indeed it is a lost virtue depends on what we mean by it. People don't seem to be in love with virtue regardless of the era when they live. The novelty of our own modernity is that humility is not even considered among the potential candidates for virtue. There is a simple explanation for it: we live in a world of me-ism, as Bellitto calls it, "an infection that makes us sick." Our departure from humility leads to what we experience every day in the media or even at home: "We live in a world not of 'I'm right and you're wrong' but of 'I'm right and you're bad.'"[2] How did we arrive here? It must have something to do with the (false) belief of our age that individuals are complete as they are, with no need from anyone else. Even this is a manifestation of our attempt to run as far as possible from one conception of humility, the act of being humiliated by others. Life with others always humbles us, either naturally, because we perceive that others are better than us in various ways, or because people want to show us that they are better, because of the same me-ism that occupies our hearts. Athens, the ideological ancestor of the Western world, has never been known for humbleness. When someone like Socrates appeared, claiming that we should do good to others, regardless of what they may do to us, the Greeks made him drink hemlock. The Romans went to Jerusalem and put Jesus on the cross—true, after Jerusalem itself rejected its prophet. Whether it is Athens or Jerusalem, people have never joyfully embraced humility, because it comes with a negation of the self. You need to be aware of your limits and humble enough to give yourself to another. There is no surprise that humility is then found in religious contexts. The lesson of the tax collector, who boasts in comparing himself with another and thus leaves unjustified, shows that one cannot have humility and judgment at the same time.

But how can one be humble and also be the "light of the world"? Such questions appear in what Bellitto calls the "medieval

2. Bellitto, *Humility*, 4.

golden age." His reading is based on balance. Some may say that it has an Aristotelian flavor, almost placing humility as a means between two extremes. Lack of humility leads to me-ism; Bellitto is clear that focusing on self can only lead to harming others and the world around you. Socrates has already expressed this wisdom: sophistry ("self-absorbed curiosity" may actually be a good translation for it) harms the sophist but also the world around him. This is because everything becomes pointless, an exercise in futility, argumentation for its own sake. Or, with a Romanian expression: a massage to a wooden leg. But on the other extreme, humility can lead to hatred of oneself. This is more difficult to understand, especially because it seems to contain an aspect of pride. Thus, he says, "An individual's gifts are useless if not shared, but this also entails a realization that a person has only one set of gifts and requires the talents of others. Humility acknowledges your own talents as well as your limits, recognizing that no one person knows it all, can do it all, or has it all."[3]

One way to express this is the paradox of learned ignorance. Abelard, Bellitto says, "knew what he didn't know, but he was confident he could find out."[4] Inquiry requires awareness of ignorance, but it also presupposes the hope that ignorance can be cured.

Of course, one can lack humility about anything: one's muscles, one's financial status, or one's spouse. Boastfulness, however, has its deepest root planted in a belief that we are self-sufficient and we need no one else to understand life. The following step is to believe that we can make the world better than it is given to us, so we are tempted to "repair" it. We can call this desire to eliminate suffering a desire to beautify the world. Exhausted by the ugliness that surrounds us, by the innumerable instances of violence, treason, or boorishness, we want to change our reality and the people belonging to it in the name of the good. .

This is the feature of all self-proclaimed saviors: they perceive the world must be in a certain way, according to their own criteria of beauty, and they don't understand your "inability" to live in it.

3. Bellitto, *Humility*, 62–63.
4. Bellitto, *Humility*, 81.

They inevitably fall into the temptation of judging their cosmos, perhaps even without realizing, from the position of the sun. The antidote to this: humility. Without it, there is no joy in the world, whether you are a "savior" or the "beneficiary" of his act. There is no higher suffering than the suffering of the one who believes that she has dedicated her life to you in her attempt to create a beautiful world in which you have to live. In her focus on the beauty that she imagines, she forgets about you, and so she remains alone, creating everything around her in a mirror, in a splendid life that clones everyone else out of her cells. The suffering is multiplied by the ungratefulness she perceives in you: "I dedicated my life to you, and you throw it in the trash by not accepting it." It is the hell that all tyrants who perceive themselves as their nations' saviors must live in. But it is also the hell that we, in our daily, small lives, can live in if our lack of humility makes us ever believe we can "fix" other human beings.

There is also another aspect of humility that appears in how others treat you: can you accept mistreatment without responding to it, without feeling justified paying back? And even if you don't pay back, can you accept it without making it evident, to the one who mistreated you and to the world, that you have been mistreated? After all, such a story is found in the same Plato. In the *Republic* (358d-361d), Glaucon, a Greek of the time, tells Socrates the story of the ring of Gyges, a story that supposedly illustrates human nature: people believe that doing wrong to benefit themselves is intrinsically good, but they avoid doing so because they fear that the repercussions are higher than the benefits. The story is about a shepherd, Gyges, who finds a miraculous ring that makes him invisible to others. The moment he realizes it, Gyges shows that the role of a shepherd—so taking care of others—is not for him. Instead, he goes to the court, seduces the king's wife, and kills the king with her help. This is how he takes over the kingdom.

Gyges's development is telling. Prior to finding the ring, he is a shepherd, so someone whose meaning is to take care of others. This requires a sense of humility, starting from the mere fact that others' needs come before yours. The ring changes Gyges and transforms him into a me-ism, to use Christopher M. Bellitto's phrase. His hubris brings death around him and pleasure for himself alone—and perhaps for the queen, but Plato is quiet on that. Glaucon, who tells this story, doesn't see the story as a transformation of a man from good to bad, but rather as a revelation of the true nature of a human being. We act properly in society because we don't have the power and the interest to act otherwise. Were we to have a ring of power, we would act the way we truly want. The story of Gyges may suggest that justice is not desired for its intrinsic qualities. The problem, though, is that it says more than this: humility is not a lost virtue; we've never had it to begin with. The few who've talked about it were portrayed as the fools of their era, regardless of whether they were our peers or our gods.

Bellitto's book surfaces in a world in which humility is not even an afterthought. This is certainly to be expected, since we are taught that we are self-sufficient and we can survive independently, as individuals. Whoever teaches something else than me-ism, a notion that may seem to describe the way we approach things superbly, is not merely different, but wrong. Humility can no longer be accepted because it tells us something opposite to the values upon which we have built our lives: it teaches us that we are not self-sufficient and we cannot live genuine human lives if we don't rely humbly on others.

The Ring of Gyges story is a powerful argument against Socrates's claim that doing good to others is among the highest goods, since it is desired both for its own sake and for the consequences it brings. With a story such as this, Glaucon attacks both aspects of Socrates's claim: doing good to others is not intrinsically good, since people act so only because they cannot do otherwise without being punished. Fearing punishment, they seem to be shepherds to others, taking care of their needs. Make the punishment disappear, and we all become wolves, feasting on the flesh of another. Our feelings of justice, and especially humility, do not come easy for us. They are contrary to our selfish nature and, paradoxically, secondary consequences of it. We help others because we are selfish: we know that, in the conditions in which we live, this is the safest approach.

But the story is not sufficient, so Socrates himself gives another example: consider two lives, the one of the most unjust and the one of the most just. The most unjust uses everyone else for his advantage, but he has honors, and all perceive him as the most just person. The most just person, on the contrary, is virtuous in all moments of his life, but he has the life of a beggar, and everyone else believes that he is unjust. Which life would you choose? Suppose that we choose the life of the just out of humility. Would we choose the same life for our children if a fairy came to their birth and placed us before this choice?

Bellitto's history shows that we would most likely not do it. This is because, regardless of whether we think of ourselves as humble, we have difficulty to genuinely accept that we are nothing else than a handful of dirt. A handful of earth. He reminds us that humility comes from humus. This is the situation of the earth, as it appears in Anthony Bloom's *Beginning to Pray*, to whom I must return. The earth . . .

> always there, always taken for granted, never remembered, always trodden on by everyone, somewhere we cast and pour out all the refuse, all we don't need. It's there, silent and accepting everything and in a miraculous way making out of all the refuse new richness in spite of corruption, transforming corruption itself into a power of life and a new possibility of creativeness, open to the sunshine, open to the rain, ready to receive any seed we sow and capable of bringing thirtyfold, sixtyfold, a hundredfold out of every seed.[5]

If humility truly is the situation of the earth, then its history is humanity's running away from it. For the earth is the place where death and life unite: we flee the former and consequently never reach the latter.

---

5. Bloom, *Beginning to Pray*, 35.

Beyond Morality

CHRISTIANITY IS OFTEN MISCONSTRUED as a religion about the good and the bad, about the righteous and the unrighteous. Do this and you will be saved. Do that and you will be damned. Described in these terms, it remains a religion of separation. How is this consistent with the image of Christ, who opens His arms on the cross as the beginning of an embrace for all?

Of course, we have the Gospel of Judgment. "Then the King will say to those on His right hand, 'Come, you blessed of My Father, inherit the kingdom prepared for you from the foundation of the world; for I was hungry and you gave Me food; I was thirsty and you gave Me drink; I was a stranger and you took Me in; I was naked and you clothed Me; I was sick and you visited Me; I was in prison and you came to Me'" (Matt 25:34–36). Such texts may give us justification to judge, to divide the world into righteous and unrighteous. But perhaps even this reminds us that we may believe we live, while in fact we are dead, embracing no one else other than ourselves, oblivious to the wounds of the others.

I think you find the essence of Christianity if you behold the two main icons of an iconostas. They guard the royal door, the entrance in the altar. On the right side, it is Christ, the God-man by nature, who has become man so man can become God (St. Athanasius). On the left side, it is Mary, the Mother of the Lord, the human being par excellence in Christianity. The human who has become god by grace, by taking upon herself giving birth to Christ.

The iconostas is the story of humanity: to love the God-man is to be a god-man, and to be a god-man is to give birth to God in you, so to decrease in order for Him to increase, to die in order to live.

Some believe that to be a supra-human you must will to become one with the Godhead. Idolatry understood as faith. A Raskolnikov. But the god-man by excellence, Mary, says simply: "Be it done unto me according to Thy word."

Christianity is not about being unrighteous or righteous. It is about being dead or alive.

Daily Involuntary Participation in Ugliness

THERE IS A SENSE in which every day of our existence is marked by our involuntary participation in ugliness: you walk on a street, a rabbit gets scared, and the rabbit runs under the wheels of a car; your gestures or habits can get someone else out of his mind, or you even fall into abominable activities, like Sonya in *Crime and Punishment*, in her participation in the world that is given to her. Still, "the world will be saved by beauty,"[1] as Dostoevsky has it.

The miracle of existence: the presence, at the same time, of ugliness and beauty. The Cross and the Resurrection. The prison and the uncreated light (Fr. George Calciu's memories). Ephemeral world and eternity.

The strongest temptation is to reject one (ugliness) to obtain the other (beauty). Or to accept the existence of only one (ugliness) because you lost hope in the existence of the other (beauty).

I used to believe that the Romanian story "Ageless Youth and Deathless Life"[2] meant that your purpose in life is to refuse your surroundings, leave them behind you, and pursue tenaciously the eternal life of the Kingdom. Here's how the story goes:

The child of an emperor and empress refuses to be born. He was to be born into leading people, and this is not attractive for the child. The emperor promises him every possible thing—dominion

---

1. Dostoevsky, *Idiot*, 402.
2. Ispirescu, "Ageless Youth," 225–32.

over lands, the most beautiful bride—but the child cries in his mother's womb, refusing to come out.

The emperor then has a moment of inspiration, and he tells the child, "Quiet, my son, and I'll give you Ageless Youth and Deathless Life."

"Ageless Youth and Deathless Life" does not presuppose leading people: the child stops crying and accepts to be born into something else than what he was naturally born into, to be the king of his people. He accepts his birth under the sign of eternity.

When he grows up, he asks his father to finally give him what he was promised at birth. Of course, a leader of people does not have such a thing to give, and so the prince leaves his home to search for the dream unto which he was born. If no one can give him "Ageless Youth and Deathless Life," then he hopes to find it on his own, outside of the realm of people.

I will not recount all his adventures. He does find the realm of ageless youth and deathless life where time disappears, and he experiences eternal joy, in the absence of other people. Still, wandering in the beautiful realm of ageless youth and deathless life (the heaven of the philosophers, the realm of Plato's Forms), he steps by mistake into the Valley of Tears, where he remembers he had a father and a mother and where he remembers he had a people. This memory awakes in him a longing for the past but also a feeling of responsibility for others. He decides to go back to the realm where he was expected to be king. The three ladies of the eternal realm tell him that nothing is waiting for him there. The wonderful horse that carried him through all the obstacles before getting to Ageless Youth and Deathless Life tells him he won't find anything when he goes back. Nevertheless, he decides to return.

They go back, and time finally catches up with the prince, his body getting older. There's nothing waiting for him: a new city is on the place of his parents' palace, and a new people lives in those lands.

The prince must not have been complete in the kingdom of Deathless Life; otherwise, he would not have returned. If this is so, then the purpose is not to refuse your surroundings and pursue tenaciously the eternal life of the Kingdom. In the Kingdom of Ageless Youth and Deathless Life, the prince could no longer be what he was created to be, a human living in the midst of his peers, taking on his responsibility, with fear and trembling. If you truly were in the realm of ageless youth and deathless life, you cannot long for your former existence, because this would mean that the kingdom of eternity is not complete. It is right for him to return to his former life, because the kingdom of eternity must be experienced while in the world of loss and suffering.

Beauty does not replace a difficult existence. Beauty gives it orientation. We live within beauty (Noica's Romanian word "întru" would be best here) by embracing whatever cross is given to us. Refusing it, like the prince refused to be born into what his life was supposed to be, cannot lead to beauty, regardless of how easy life may seem to become.

Moments of Travel with Dostoevsky and Elder Cleopa

My father has terminal cancer.

☙

I left home to go home.

☙

There are so many cemeteries on the way from Făgăraș to the airport. In the speed of the car, I think I see one with soldiers fallen during WWI. So many young people who could not be mourned by their unborn children . . . Still, they are my "parents." I can mourn them. Or I can rejoice in them. I carry them with me, whether I want it or not. I am most aware of it when I see the cross from my own tomb before my eyes. "The highest wisdom of human beings?" asked Elder Cleopa. He answered, "Death! Death! Death!"

☙

"Only in the light of Dostoevsky's fundamental artistic task [. . .] can one begin to understand the profound organic cohesion, consistency and wholeness of Dostoevsky's poetics." Bakhtin is correct: there is consistency and wholeness in Dostoevsky's work. Perhaps because of his dialogism as well, but for sure for one other reason: death is the one that gives consistency to his world. Everything in Dostoevsky's writings can be understood as long as we begin with the end, the inevitable end of all his characters, the inevitable end of all human beings. Dostoevsky's world is cohesive inasmuch as it is governed by death. Paradoxically, some may say, but most naturally, I would say, it is this death that gives light and brilliance to all human beings.

I got on the plane. There's a lady next to me. She has two toddlers. "She will cry," she says, pointing to her daughter. She's probably one year old, and she's so full of life. She has no inhibitions and makes sure that everyone around her is aware of her presence. Two seats in front of me, a young adult is playing on his phone. His earbuds in his ears, he's completely closed to everyone around him. How many prayers does he carry with him? Do his parents' thoughts embrace him on his journey?

A few years ago, I went to Fr. Roman Braga's funeral. The day before the entombment, the church at the Dormition Monastery was full: clergy and people, all brought together by their love for Fr. Roman. His corpse was laying in the middle of the church, facing the altar, and we were all singing: "Christ is Risen from the death, trampling down death by death, and upon those in the tomb bestowing life."

The act of the crucifixion was so serious, authentic, and complete that even the apostles and disciples were convinced that the man hanging on the middle piece of wood would not rise again. If they hadn't been so shaken in their faith, Luke and Cleopas would not have walked so cheerlessly, shuffling their feet on the way to Emmaus; they would have recognized their teacher immediately and would not have been so surprised when they understood who He was. (They had felt so embarrassed, so deceived, that they had asked the first passerby they came across, a stranger, to not leave them alone, to stay with them).[1]

The little girl fell asleep, and so my seat neighbor enjoys some peace and quiet. We all do.

We can be so separated, and still so united. Flying together to various "homes," flying together to personal deaths. Still, each one of us is embraced by so many angels. Just like this girl, whose mother keeps her in her arms, without complaining for one moment, although she could not move for an hour. She only smiles, looking at her girl. Blessed are those whose arms are other people's seatbelts. And blessed are those who have their seatbelts on for the moment of landing.

---

1. Steinhardt, *Journal of Joy*, 84–85.

Bibliography

Aesop. *Aesop's Fables*. Translated by Laura Gibbs. Oxford: Oxford University Press, 2002.
Bakhtin, M. M. *The Dialogic Imagination: Four Essays*. Edited by Michael Holquist. Translated by Caryl Emerson and Michael Holquist. Austin: University of Texas Press, 2002.
———. *Problems of Dostoevsky's Poetics*. Edited and translated by Caryl Emerson. Minneapolis: University of Minnesota Press, 1984.
Beckett, Samuel. *Waiting for Godot*. Translated by Samuel Beckett. New York: Grove, 1982.
Bellitto, Christopher M. *Humility: The Secret History of a Lost Virtue*. Washington, DC: Georgetown University Press, 2023.
Blaga, Lucian. "Eu nu strivesc corola de minuni a lumii." In *Opera Poetică*. București: Humanitas, 1995, 33.
Bloom, Anthony. *Beginning to Pray*. Paulist Press, 1970.
Boca, Arsenie. *Living Words*. Translated by Octavian Gabor and Fr. Gregory Allard. Charisma, 2014.
Brădățan, Costică. *In Praise of Failure: Four Lessons in Humility*. Cambridge, MA: Harvard University Press, 2023.
Calciu, George. *Interviews, Homilies, and Talks*. Saint Herman of Alaska Brotherhood, 2010.
Dostoevsky, Fyodor. *Crime and Punishment*. Translated by J. Coulson. Oxford: Oxford University Press, 2008.
———. *Devils*. Translated by Michael R. Katz. Oxford: Oxford University Press, 2008.
———. *The Idiot*. Translated by Alan Myers. Oxford: Oxford University Press, 2008.
———. *The Karamazov Brothers*. Translated by Ignat Avsey. Oxford: Oxford University Press, 1994.
Eliade, Mircea. *The Sacred and the Profane*. Translated by Willard R. Trask. Orlando: Harcourt, 1987.

Emerson, Caryl. "Mikhail Bakhtin." In *The Oxford Handbook of Russian Religious Thought*, edited by Caryl Emerson, George Pattison, and Randall A. Poole, 608–26. Oxford: Oxford University Press, 2020.

Ispirescu, Petre. "Ageless Youth and Deathless Life." Translated by Elena Gabor. In Constantin Noica, *The Romanian Sentiment of Being*, 225–32. Translated by Octavian and Elena Gabor. Punctum, 2022.

Kundera, Milan. *The Book of Laughter and Forgetting*. Translated by Aaron Asher. Harper Perennial Classics, 1999.

Levinas, Emmanuel. *In the Time of the Nations*. Translated by Michael B. Smith. London: Continuum, 2007.

———. *Otherwise than Being or Beyond Essence*. Translated by Alphonso Lingis. Pittsburgh: Duquesne University Press, 2002.

Lewis, C. S. "Preface." In Saint Athanasius, *On the Incarnation*, 11–17. Translated by John Behr. Yonkers, NY: St. Vladimir's Seminary Press, 2011.

Monk Moise. *Do Not Avenge Us: Testimonies About the Sufferings of the Romanians Deported from Bessarabia to Siberia*. Translated by Octavian Gabor. Citrus Heights, CA: Reflection, 2016.

Noica, Constantin. *Becoming Within Being*. Translated by Alistair Ian Blyth. Milwaukee: Marquette University Press, 2009.

———. *Jurnal filozofic*. Bucharest: Humanitas, 1990.

———. *Pray for Brother Alexander*. Translated by Octavian Gabor. Punctum, 2018.

Philip, Metropolitan, and Joseph Allen. *Meeting the Incarnate God: From the Human Depths to the Mystery of Fidelity*. Brookline, MA: Holy Cross Orthodox Press, 2009.

Plato. *Sophist*. Translated by Seth Benardete. Chicago: University of Chicago Press, 1986.

Solzhenitsyn, Aleksandr. *The Gulag Archipelago*. Vol II. Translated by Thomas P. Whitney. New York: Harper Perennial, 2007.

Stăniloae, Dumitru. *Eternity and Time*. Oxford: SLG, 2001.

Steinhardt, Nicolae *The Journal of Joy*. Translated by Paul Boboc. Yonkers, NY: St. Vladimir's Seminary Press, 2024.

Tolstoy, Leo. "The Two Old Men." In *The Death of Ivan Ilyich and Other Stories*, 3–23. Translated by Nicolas Pasternak Slater. Oxford: Oxford University Press, 2015.

Yannaras, Christos. *Person and Eros*. Translated by Norman Russell. Brookline, MA: Holy Cross Orthodox Press, 2007.

www.ingramcontent.com/pod-product-compliance
Lightning Source LLC
Chambersburg PA
CBHW071609170426
43196CB00034B/2269

www.ingramcontent.com/pod-product-compliance
Lightning Source LLC
Chambersburg PA
CBHW071609170426
43196CB00034B/2281